BUILD
YOUR OWN
BOAT

BUILD YOUR OWN BOAT

Percy W. Blandford

DOVER PUBLICATIONS, INC.
Mineola, New York

CONTENTS

ILLUSTRATIONS

LINE DRAWINGS IN TEXT

INTRODUCTION

BOATING is rapidly becoming a major outdoor activity, and the enjoyment and satisfaction to be gained by getting afloat can be increased considerably by first building your boat. An old-time boat builder had to be a highly skilled craftsman, but modern materials have made possible simpler, although often better, methods of construction, so that, if the right design is chosen, a moderately skilled handyman with a very sketchy tool-kit can build a boat which will be perfectly satisfactory. At the same time there is still scope for craftsmanship and the more ambitious worker can exercise his skill. In other constructional work much of the joy of hand craftsmanship has gone, but in this mass-production high-pressure world building a boat of your own allows you to savour the satisfaction of achieving something with your own hands.

There has been a quiet revolution in boat building. This means that methods of less than ten years ago, which were recommended practice then, have had to give way to other methods which make use of more modern materials. This book is concerned with methods used today, with reference to traditional techniques only where they are still acceptable in the light of modern knowledge. The author is well aware that boat owners tend to be traditionally minded and want a 'boat that looks like a boat', so that changes take some time to become accepted tradition. After thirty-five years building and using boats of all types he hopes he can claim to have a feeling for boats of an acceptable form.

The author is a designer specialising in the smallest craft, who builds with his own hands a prototype before releasing plans for the use of amateur and professional boat builders. His designs are used all over the world, and the number of boats built to them is well over 50,000. He has had personal experience of all methods of construction. Based on this he has included the essential information which anyone building a boat is likely to need. The aim is to offer a practical book, shorn of inessentials and out-of-date techniques.

The author hopes to be designing and building boats for a long time. If anyone has any problems concerning boat building or the choice of designs he is willing to attempt to provide an answer if written to at the forwarding address: BM/BOAT, London WC1.

All of the photographs and drawings in this book are by the author.

I

MATERIALS

BOATS have been built of a great many materials, but wood has always been more popular than anything else. Unless an amateur is especially skilled in working other materials he should choose wood. It is particularly suitable for boats and has the advantage of being easy to work. If the right woods are chosen a boat can be expected to have a long life. With modern methods, no part of quite a large amateur-built boat need be very heavy or need complicated or expensive tools or equipment to work it.

Not every wood is suitable for boat building. Even some woods which are quite satisfactory ashore are unsuitable in damp conditions afloat. Designers usually include suggestions for suitable woods with plans, and these should be followed. By far the most popular wood for boat building is mahogany, although this name really covers a great variety of woods within the same family. Teak is the traditional high-class boat-building wood, but it is heavy, difficult to work and expensive. Oak is not used afloat as much as ashore, although it has its uses. At one time English elm was popular for planking, but it is only suitable for a boat left afloat and is not often used today. Rock elm is a different wood, which is used because it is suitable for bending. Ash also bends well, but is not as durable.

Softwoods in general are not very durable, but they are used because of lightness. Sitka spruce, which is rarely used ashore, is the most popular wood for spars and similar things because of its strength in relation to its light weight. Common deal and the woods, such as parana pine, which are substituted for it in carpentry ashore, have their uses for internal work in a boat, but they are not suitable for external parts.

An increasingly large variety of attractive hardwoods are being imported under the collective name of 'Empire hardwoods'. Each visit to a timber yard produces new names, so it is difficult to keep track of names and details, but if the characteristics of a wood are similar to one recommended by the designer it may be used. Some details of these woods are given in Appendix A. Of course, for internal work in a cabin boat, where conditions are little different from in a house, woods may be chosen for the sake of their appearance.

The wood development which has brought about a revolution in the boat-building industry, and made the home building of boats much simpler, is the production of plywood, which for all practical purposes is fully waterproof. The wartime development of waterproof synthetic resin glues has made this possible. Most marine-grade plywood is made from veneers of mahogany or wood of similar appearance. In Britain it is marked 'B.S.S. 1088'. This is the British Standard Specification indicating that the plywood has been manufactured to the boat-building standard. It may have other markings indicating the grade of glue and other properties of the plywood, but the important mark is 'B.S.S. 1088'. A plywood made with the same glue, but of a quality intended for outside work in house building, is marked 'exterior grade'. If marine grade is unavailable this may have to be used in some countries. Not all marine and exterior plywood is made of mahogany. Douglas fir is used in America and is available in other countries. This is rather coarse and does not take a good finish, but it will produce a light boat.

Timber for boat building should be the best of its type. Some woods with minor flaws and imperfections may still be satisfactory for many jobs ashore, but it needs to be selected material for structural parts of a boat. This means that it is best to buy from a timber yard specialising in boat-building timbers if possible. Wood should be correctly seasoned. This means that sap has been dried out, either naturally or by a forced method, so that it remains with a certain moisture content. Excessive drying may be as much a fault as lack of seasoning.

Timber merchants catering for house builders may sell wood to 'nominal sizes'. This means that the size quoted is the sawn size and machine planing reduces it by about $\frac{1}{8}$ in. Measuring in this way is unsuitable for boat building and wood should be specified as 'planed all round to finished sizes'. Sizes quoted in plans are actual and not nominal. Of course, buying timber machine planed ensures accuracy and reduces labour.

British marine-grade plywood is normally available in 8 ft. × 4 ft. sheets, but other sizes are sometimes available, and some firms will scarf sheets to make up any length. Actually 8 ft. × 4 ft. is the largest sheet that can conveniently be handled by one man and joints in construction are not difficult to make (see Chapter 4). Thicknesses may be metric or English measure. Metric measure allows a finer variation in thicknesses (about 25·4 mm to 1 in.). Except for canoes, skins of boats are not usually less than $\frac{1}{4}$ in. (6 mm). In their code of practice issued to members the Ship and Boat Builders' National Federation does not approve less than $\frac{1}{4}$ in. for even the smallest boats. In this book there are no recommendations which would be contrary to this code.

Synthetic resin glues allow wood joints in boats to be made with confidence. Where suitable cramping can be arranged joints can be made without metal fastenings. In production work glues which can be set rapidly by the application of heat allow very quick building. An example is glued clinker construction, where the glue between overlapped planks is set in a very short time, using a strip electric heater. However, this needs specialised equipment and glues which set in a few hours at normal temperatures are of more use to amateur boat builders.

The synthetic resin glues available to amateurs vary in their method of use, although the results all give adequate strength. There may be a syrup, or a powder to mix with water to make a syrup. Aerolite 300 and 306 are examples. The syrup is applied to one surface and a liquid hardener applied to the other. Setting time depends on temperature and the grade of hardener. Another popular type has a powder hardener already mixed with the powder glue (Cascamite One-shot). Sufficient is mixed with water for use in an hour or so. Any unused surplus will harden and be useless. Another type (Beetle A) has a liquid hardener which is added to the glue syrup just before use, and the mixture must be used within an hour or so, depending on temperature. Once set, none of these glues can be softened again. If an attempt is made to break a properly glued joint the wood fibres will give way rather than the glue line.

Before the coming of synthetic resins, casein glue was used in boat building. This is only water-resistant and will lose its strength if it becomes soaked with water. It is still available and has uses ashore, but should not be used for modern boat building.

There have been attempts to use some of the great variety of plastics for boat building. Glass-reinforced plastics (better known as 'glass fibre') is successful (see Chapter 9), but, at the time of writing, none of the other plastics has become acceptable for boat hulls and structure, although many find similar uses to those in houses in cabin boats. Related to plastics are the concrete hulls produced commercially. Of course, the material is not the same as used for constructional work ashore, but is something of a trade secret and is not available for amateur use.

Not many amateurs are likely to want to build metal boats. Facilities and equipment needed are more than an amateur will possess. Boats are built of steel, either welded or riveted. Ideally the hulls are finished by galvanising. More easily worked are aluminium alloys. These should be salt-water-resistant types. Hulls built of this material are expensive, but they need little maintenance and are very strong.

Fabrics are used in boat building for several purposes. Canoes and folding boats may have fabric skins and inflatable craft are almost entirely fabric. The Royal Navy has a system of grading canvas by numbers, but most ordinary canvas available from suppliers is graded by its weight per square yard. Dinghy sails may be only 1 oz. or 2 oz., while covers and awnings would more likely be 12 oz. or 15 oz. For most purposes it is advisable to buy canvas which has been proofed by the makers. This adds to its weight and may shrink the canvas slightly, so a 15 oz. canvas, 36 in. wide, may in fact be 16 oz. or more and perhaps only 35 in. wide.

Rubberised fabrics have been used for many purposes, but ordinary rubber is affected by sun and grease. Synthetic rubbers are more often used today. P.V.C. fabric is the most commonly used plastic fabric. Canvas coated both sides with this plastic makes a good canoe skin, cruiser cockpit canopy or boat cover.

Synthetic resin glues are unsuitable for fabrics, partly because they may not adhere to all of them, but mainly because they set absolutely rigid. There is no flexible adhesive which is suitable for all fabrics. Rubber solution, as used for tyres, may be used on rubber, but it is unsuitable for anything else. Black reclaim cement, such as Bostik C, will stick canvas to itself or to wood. For plastics it is necessary to follow the makers' recommendations. For a few plastics there are no satisfactory adhesives and a few can only be joined by welding, using local heat.

Akin to glues and adhesives are stoppings. They fill holes and seams, but do not provide strength. Some household stoppings are not waterproof and should be avoided. Plastic wood (with the pear-drop smell) is waterproof, but it is better to use a marine stopping. A rigid stopping, obtainable in a colour to match the wood, should be used over screw heads and similar places. Brummer is an example. When set, this can be sanded down and painted or varnished with the surrounding wood. In places where there is a possibility of movement in a seam, due to expansion and contraction of the wood, a flexible stopping should be used. There is a flexible version of Brummer, and Seelastik is another well-known type. This sets sufficiently firm to be painted over, but remains slightly flexible.

At one time boat builders made up stoppings for caulking and other purposes, but now suitable plastic-based materials are available. Similarly, marine glue was always used for the joints between deck planks. This is a stopping and not a glue in the accepted sense and is still available. It has to be heated and poured into the seams. One of the other flexible stoppings will be found more convenient to use.

Screws and nails are used in large quantities in even a small wooden boat. Domestic iron fastenings would soon rust. There are a few places in some boats where unprotected iron is used, but the majority of fastenings have to be resistant to water, particularly salt water. An increasingly large variety of alloys are being used for fastenings.

Steel nails and screws may be protected by galvanising (deposit of zinc). This leaves a rough surface—too rough for small screws—and the zinc may be removed by hammer or screwdriver. There are smooth zinc-plated screws also available. These fastenings have possibilities for internal work, but they are only used for places in contact with water for the cheapest work and are not advised for use by amateurs.

The most commonly used screws are brass. In practice they generally prove satisfactory, especially when used to supplement glued joints, but ordinary brass screws have two faults. They are rather brittle and there is a risk of thinner screws shearing off when being driven. Brass is an alloy of copper and zinc. Salt water may cause the zinc to be eaten away, weakening the screw.

Better screws are gunmetal (alloy of copper and tin), monel metal, silicon bronze and other special alloys; all of which tend to be more expensive. Screws are sold by their length, from the surface of the wood, and a gauge number denoting thickness. Thickness increases as the gauge numbers get bigger. Countersunk heads are usual for most purposes (fig 1A). Round heads (fig. 1B) may look better on some fittings, while for such things as hinges screwed to the surface, a raised head (fig. 1C) looks better. In a

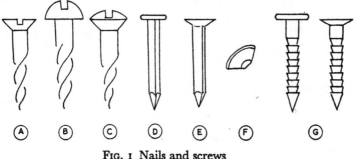

Fig. 1 Nails and screws

plywood dinghy most screws will be less than gauge 10. Gauge 4 is about ⅛ in. diameter, while gauge 8 is ⅛ in.

Traditional boat-building nails are copper and square in section. They may have flat (fig. 1D) or countersunk (fig. 1E) heads. They are sold by weight and described by their length and gauge number. The gauge used is the Standard Wire Gauge, in which the thickness decreases as the numbers increase. Common gauges for small-boat work are between 10 and 16. These nails are also used as rivets; the end being driven through a rove, cut off and burred over (see Chapter 4). A rove is a copper conical washer with a hole small enough to need force to push it over the nail (fig. 1F). Copper has a good resistance to salt water, but it is soft and not as strong as many alloys. Its softness makes it suitable for riveting.

Between nails and screws are barbed ring nails (fig. 1G). They are driven like nails, but have the holding power of screws. Two types are commonly available—Gripfast (silicon bronze alloy) and Anchorfast (monel alloy). These nails are sold in packets by number or in larger quantities by weight. They are described by their length and gauge number (Standard Wire Gauge as ordinary nails). Heads may be flat or countersunk. For fixing plywood panels, using these nails instead of screws can represent a considerable saving in time, particularly if working single-handed.

Paints and varnishes used on boats should be marine types. Household finishes may not stand up to wet conditions. There are several paint manufacturers specialising in marine finishes and they issue booklets describing their products and giving recommendations for various purposes on boats. On a particular boat it is advisable to have all the products of one maker, following their recommendations. This is particularly important with primer, undercoat and topcoat on new work.

Nearly all marine finishes are synthetic. Paints and

varnishes made with natural resins were often very sensitive to climatic changes when being applied. Those made from synthetic materials are more tolerant of conditions. When a boat is kept afloat on salt water even the best ordinary finishes may not last through a season. There are special finishes, which are more durable, and more expensive. Polyurethane paint and varnish may be obtained with two parts, which have to be mixed before applying, rather like synthetic resin glue. This produces a harder and more durable surface. A one-part polyurethane finish is also available, but this is not as good.

Varnishwork looks good, but it is more difficult to keep in good condition. The smallest boats may be entirely varnished, but it is more usual for larger boats to have their hulls painted. A boat which is kept out of the water when not in use may have its hull painted the same all over, but a boat which is kept afloat may need anti-fouling paint below the water-line. This reduces marine growth, but the most effective anti-fouling paints only continue to work if kept wet, so they are unsuitable for a boat which is hauled out. Marine paints tend to be expensive, so their correct choice and use are important.

Hardboard is a manufactured board, made from wood and commonly available in sheets 8 ft. × 4 ft. The usual thickness is ⅛ in., but thicker boards are also available. It does not have much use afloat, but most makers produce a water-resistant type, often called 'oil-tempered', which can be used in the internal fitting of cabins and for similar jobs. The smooth-face side takes paint well. Oil-tempered hardboard has been used for the skins of small boats. It may produce a lighter and cheaper boat than plywood, but the boat has to be given careful use and its life is not likely to be as long. For the majority of purposes using oil-tempered hardboard in place of plywood for a boat skin is inadvisable.

2

CHOICE OF BOAT

ALTHOUGH this is primarily a practical book, some knowledge of the theory behind boat designing will help when choosing a boat to build. Boat designing is as much an art as a science. While a designer should know something of science and mathematics as applied to boats, it is a fact that some of the most successful boats have been designed by men with an eye for a curve, who probably did not resort to mathematics until checking their design after it had been drawn. What looks right, usually is right. A successful boat should be a thing of beauty.

Speed through the water is related to length on the water-line more than to anything else. A long boat, possibly of inferior design, will be faster than a much shorter boat, even if the latter has much better lines. This applies to boats intended to remain in the water—those which lift and plane with part of their hull out of the water will be discussed later.

Another consideration affecting speed is skin friction. Besides having the skin as smooth and clean as possible there is an advantage in reducing the wetted area. The shape which gives the minimum wetted area has a semi-circular cross-section near the middle of the boat (fig. 2A). Racing skiffs and canoes may have this section, but stability is negligible. Stability may be provided by having

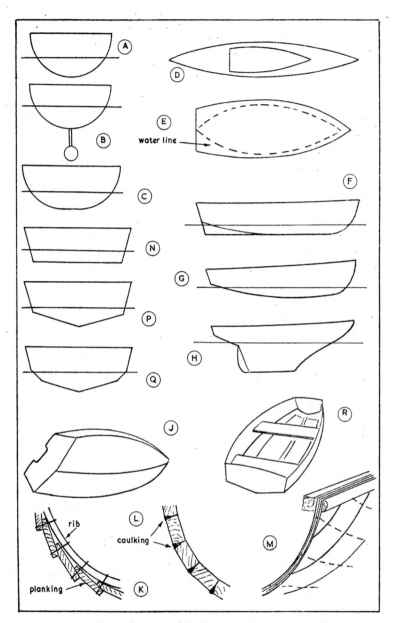

FIG. 2. Boat shapes and basic methods of construction

a deep weighted keel (fig. 2B), but this also increases the wetted area, causing drag. Instead, in dinghies and other light boats, stability is obtained by flattening the curve (fig. 2C). The greater the area of nearly flat bottom around the middle of the boat, the more stable will it be. A certain amount of extra drag due to the increased wetted area has to be accepted in return for the stability.

The shape of a fish gives a clue to the streamlined shape which the underwater part of a boat should be. Abrupt angles and changes of shape must be avoided. Lines should run to a point, fore and aft. A canoe or kayak obviously has this shape (fig. 2D), but many small boats have transoms at the stern, and a pram dinghy has one also at the bow. When loaded no more than intended by the designer these transoms should be above the water-line, and the underwater lines will still run to a point, which may not be very sharp in a tubby, short dinghy (fig. 2E). The lines of a dinghy should be like a boat with a pointed stern cut off above the water-line, if the best speed is to be obtained. Of course, in a little boat whose main function is as a load carrier for ferrying a short distance to a larger craft, any hope of speedy lines has to be abandoned.

If the keel line is long and straight when viewed from the side (fig. 2F) the boat will have considerable directional stability (i.e. it will hold its course very well). This can be excessive and turning the boat quickly may be almost impossible. To give manœuvrability the keel may be rockered (swept up towards the ends) (fig. 2G). This is desirable in a sailing boat, as it allows quick turning when tacking.

A racing sailing dinghy may have its water-line almost the same length as the overall length to get the greatest benefit from a long water-line. In choppy water this can result in much spray or solid water over the bow. A decked yacht will have overhanging ends so that the water-line is much shorter than the overall length (fig. 2H). As the boat pitches the overhangs give extra buoyancy to bring the boat back level.

With sufficient power it is possible to make a boat lift partly above the surface so that it is supported on only a small area of bottom at the stern. This is called planing. A boat capable of planing has a very broad flat area of bottom extending almost the same width from amidships to the stern (fig. 2J and plate 1). A planing hull is not usually very comfortable or efficient at speeds less than planing. Some sailing dinghies are designed to plane under certain conditions, but the successful design of a sailing-boat hull capable both of planing and performing well when not planing is a skilled job.

For sea-kindliness there is no shape as good as the rounded bottom. In bad weather and rough water this is the shape which can keep going and be the least uncomfortable. Not all methods of construction can be used to obtain the compound curves necessary, and the shapes used may have to be a compromise because of the limitations of materials.

Round-bottomed wooden hulls traditionally have been made in several ways, building the skin up with many narrow strips. Instructions for some of these methods are given in subsequent chapters, but the differences are illustrated here. Clinker (or clench, or lap-strake) has planks laid fore-and-aft, with the upper overlapping the lower (fig. 2K). The method is used for general-purpose boats up to 30 ft. or more in length. It tends to be rather wasteful of timber. A smoother skin with lengthwise planks is carvel construction (fig. 2L). Several ways of joining the planks are used, but the result is a flush skin.

Using several layers of veneer joined with synthetic resin glue is really making a piece of plywood in the shape

of a boat (fig. 2M). It is cheap and makes a good hull
without much internal structure, but a mould has to be
made first, and this makes it more suitable for quan-
tity-production than for building one-off. There is no
settled name for the method, which may be 'moulded
veneer', 'hot moulded' or 'cold moulded' (depending on
the method of setting the glue). Glass fibre may also be
used to make round-bottomed boats, or boats of any
shape, but much work has to be put into making a mould
first.

Sheet plywood cannot be given a double curvature,
except to a very limited extent, so it cannot be used for
round-bottom boats. Instead, to allow the plywood sheets
to curve in their length the cross-section is arranged with
straight lines. Simplest is a flat-bottomed boat (fig. 2N).
This is very stable and easy to build, but it cannot be
given very good lines and performance in broken water is
poor. The next step is to have a V bottom. The 'hard
chine' form is common in boats intended for amateur
construction (fig. 2P). The chine is the angle between the
side and the bottom. This form also lends itself to the
design of a planing bottom and high-speed planing boats
are often of this shape, even if planked.

A carefully designed hard-chine hull may be reasonably sea-kindly, but a step towards the round bottom is to
cut off the chines, with a further straight line in the
section at each side. This is called 'double chine' (fig. 2Q).
In fact the method of building is no more difficult than the
single hard-chine form and the result is a better hull for
rough-water conditions.

The newcomer usually tends to expect the capacity of
a boat to be greater than it is. Compared with a caravan
of similar overall dimensions, the shaping of a boat reduces the capacity to perhaps half. The lines necessary
for a sailing-boat hull reduce capacity to less than that of

a motor cruiser of similar overall size. It is possible to have a dinghy as small as 6 ft. long, but this will only carry one, except for very short distances. At 8 ft. it is possible to carry two, or even three, but there will be little comfort. Boats up to this length are usually prams (fig. 2R) which give better load carrying than if there is a stem. They are quite satisfactory if designed so that the bow board is above the water.

General-purpose dinghies, whether for rowing, outboard motor or sail, are more often 10 ft. or 12 ft. long. A normally proportioned boat of this size allows moving about without rocking being too disconcerting, there is room for three or four to sit in reasonable comfort and the size is sufficient to be safe in moderately rough water. Sail is used on boats shorter than this, but a lively performance is more likely with these bigger boats. It is even better on a length of 14 ft. or more, and many racing dinghies with high-speed performances are 16 ft. to 20 ft.

The word 'dinghy' is difficult to define, but it is a mainly open boat. If the boat has seating, wheel steering and accommodation rather like an open car, it is usually called a 'runabout'. Its motor may be inboard or outboard. Usually a runabout has a hull intended for planing. It is possible to seat four in reasonable comfort in a runabout about 11 ft. long, but the sporty and more comfortable craft tend to be nearer 14 ft. long.

The shortest hull on which it is reasonable to put a cabin is 14 ft. long, and on this size it is only a simple shelter in which it may be possible to sit almost on the bottom boards. At 16 ft. it is possible to have two bunks, cooking gear and simple amenities in a motor cruiser, but the same thing in a sailing boat would need at least 17 ft. overall. What must be guarded against is having too long a cabin. Plenty of open space is needed for handling the boat. It may be possible to sleep more on temporary beds in the cockpit under an awning, but if permanent bunks are to be provided for four adults, with space for clothing, cooking, etc., the length needs to be upwards of 20 ft.

Standing headroom in a small cabin boat is impossible without carrying the cabin to excessive heights. This gives increased windage, which may spoil the performance of a boat and can be a nuisance even when canal cruising. Sitting headroom on the bunks can be comfortable, but quite a large cruiser is needed to give standing headroom under a cabin top of reasonable height.

The smallest boats are quite cheap to build and it is easy to be misled into estimating costs of larger boats proportional only to length, but this is very far from being so. As length increases so do all other dimensions. Sizes of materials have to be greater to provide sufficient strength and the method of building a larger boat has to involve processes not included in a small boat. Built from scratch a simple plywood 6 ft. pram dinghy may cost about £10. An 11 ft. runabout, in basic form, may cost £40 without engine. Similarly the material for a 16ft. cruiser, with just the cabin, bunk framing and the basic woodwork completed, may be around £150. A sailing boat, ready to sail, is likely to cost nearly double the price of a rowing or outboard boat of the same length.

The cheapest way to build a boat is to obtain a plan and build from scratch. A schedule of material will be provided with the plan. Several firms specialise in supplying materials for well-known designs and it is possible to buy material as needed and avoid having to make one large payment at the start. By shopping around it is often possible to economise by getting materials from various sources. Many amateur builders get the greatest satisfaction out of building in this way. A further way to economise is for several builders to buy materials collectively. Complete sheets of plywood are cheaper per square foot than cut pieces. Other things may be cheaper as the result of bulk buying.

Many firms sell kits. In a kit some of the work is done for you—the amount varies between suppliers, and this should be taken into account when comparing kit prices. Such things as frames, stem and transom should be cut out. This may be just to the outline or all bevels and slots may be cut. Sometimes minor assemblies come already made. A kit may include all glue and fastenings. It may consist of wood parts only.

Where time is short, or the builder has doubts about his ability, a kit may be worth while. Some kit makers claim that as the result of bulk buying they can produce a kit as cheaply as the amateur can buy the material only. To a certain extent this may be so, but anyone intending to build from a kit must expect the boat to cost more than if built from scratch. How much more depends on how much work the kit maker has done for you.

There are firms who supply hulls complete, usually with the material to complete the boat. This may be the only way of getting a boat of a particular type if the hull has to be glass fibre or moulded veneer, but for a plywood hull there is little point in most amateurs paying someone else to make the hull unless building time and space are very short, or the boat is very big. Building a large cruiser can be very time-consuming if the work is to be done in spare time, and a professionally made hull gives a good start. Of course, a complete hull is some way towards a complete boat, and this has to be paid for.

There are a great many boats of all types about—more than sufficient to provide any man with a boat to meet his needs. A very large number of boats, to designs which have become quite well known, are only available as complete boats. Many others are only available as kits from particular boat builders, who provide instructions for completing the boat from their kit, but who will not, sell plans only. Plans only are available for many boats. These are by designers who are not also trying to sell you materials or kits, although usually other firms are authorised to make kits to suit the plans. Several yachting magazines sponsor designs and sell plans. The numbers of boats built by amateurs to some of these magazine-sponsored plans runs into many thousands.

Properly designed and built boats keep their value for a considerable time. It is not unknown for a boat to be worth more after ten years than when it was new. This applies to boats of acceptable form and construction. A boat which is so unconventional as to be a freak, or something in its construction is so unorthodox, due to ignorance or experiment, that it is not acceptable boat-building practice, will have little resale value and may even be difficult to give away. It is very frustrating to have to finally break up something on which was lavished much misguided care. There are many pitfalls in boat designing and the beginner is advised not to attempt to design his own boat, but to accept a design by an expert and follow it—at least in all major respects.

3

TOOLS

BOAT BUILDING today is mainly light woodworking. Gone are the days of starting with large pieces of timber, much of which had to be cut to waste to produce a solid-shaped part. This had to be done with large and special hand tools. Instead, modern glues and plywood permit built-up structures which are at least as good, but the wood used is in light sections and the tools needed are proportionately simpler and lighter. This applies to amateur boat building up to moderate-sized cruisers. It is not until really large craft are contemplated that the amateur boat builder needs to consider tools of a more ambitious type.

Many people succeed in building small boats with very sketchy tool kits. If a boat kit is purchased from a supplier who cuts all bevels and prefabricates as much as possible very few tools are needed to finish the job. Even when building from scratch it is usual to buy all wood ready planed to size so that heavier planes and saws are rarely needed. Obviously there is an advantage in having plenty of tools. Work will progress quicker and accuracy may sometimes be more easily obtained. If tools are few and facilities far from ideal things may be rather more difficult and time on the job may be greater.

Tools should be regarded as an investment. There are

bargains to be had and sometimes a cheap tool does the job as well as a more costly one, but in general you get what you pay for and the best tools are the most expensive. Most of the tools required are those which are basic to most branches of woodworking. Some manufacturers frequently produce special tools, dual-purpose ones, or others incorporating some special feature. These often look suspiciously like an attempt to boost sales. The value of anything new should be weighed up against the traditional article before buying it specially. That does not mean, of course, that some new tools are not improvements—there have been many new tools which are worth while, as will be seen later in the chapter.

A variety of saws are needed. A blunt saw is frustrating, and the difference between a cheap one and a dear one is in the quality of the steel, which really means the length of time the teeth will remain sharp. A hand saw of moderate size (about 18 in.) with fine teeth (about ten per inch) will cut plywood without breaking it excessively and can be used on most boat-building timbers (fig. 3A). For finer work a 12 in. tenon saw with teeth no coarser than fourteen per inch is a useful tool (fig. 3B). The professional favours the extra weight of a brass back, although it is more costly than a steel back.

Keyhole and compass saws are not of much value, although jobs may be found for them if already possessed. The hand tool for curves in plywood and light timber is a coping saw (fig. 3C). This has replaceable blades which can be arranged to cut on the push or the pull stroke. The rather cumbersome bow saw has its adherents, but it is not worth buying specially.

Small power saws are useful. A small portable circular saw may take the place of the hand saw for many purposes. This may be one having a motor built in, or a unit which attaches to an electric drill. Even more useful for

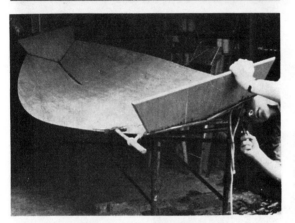

PLATE 3

The bottom of this small pram dinghy is sprung to shape with a post tightened with folding wedges. The second side is about to be fitted

PLATE 4

The bottom of this Goblin sailing dinghy is made from one piece, but the ends are given shape by being slit and sprung in. The hammer is through a rope used as a Spanish windlass

PLATE 5

A typical clinker-built pram dinghy, with a solid gunwale and grown knees. Bottom boards are sprung to shape

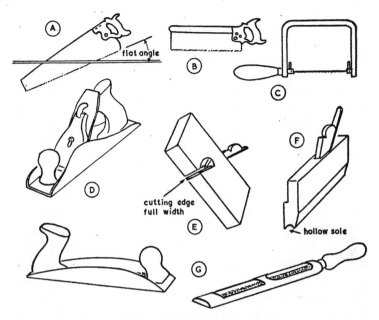

FIG. 3. Saws and planes

many boats is a power jigsaw, which cuts curves as well as straight lines in plywood and solid wood up to about $\frac{3}{4}$ in. Anyone tackling a bigger boat will appreciate a bandsaw, but its cost is not justified or necessary if one small boat is the only woodworking project contemplated.

When wood has been sawn to shape it is usually necessary to smooth it or bring it accurately to size by planing or some other process. A steel smoothing plane of the well-known Stanley pattern, about size 4, is the most commonly used plane in boat building (fig. 3D), with its lever and screw blade adjustment setting is soon mastered. If no other plane is available the adjustable throat allows it to be used for fine finishing cuts or set to remove large shavings. However, for removing wood quickly a wood jack plane is the correct tool, but its rather crude method of setting with a hammer needs a little experience to master. The longer trying plane, either steel or wood, is the tool for working long straight edges, but it need not be regarded as essential.

When fitting plywood panels a steel block plane is worth having. It is cheap, although it is worth paying extra for a screw adjustment. It is used in one hand, and its low-angled blade trims plywood neatly. For double-chine construction and some other jobs a plane is needed with its blade the full width of the sole. It need not be very wide and the usual tool is a rebate plane, either steel or wood (fig. 3E). If it has stops for width and depth of cut it is called a fillister. The stops are not needed for work on the skin, but they may be useful when tackling the internal joinery of a cabin boat. A tool which the author finds useful, but which is now difficult to buy, is a narrow plane called a 'round' (fig. 3F). With its partner, called a 'hollow', it was once included in a craftsman's tool-kit for working mouldings. In boat building the 'round' provides the quickest means of taking off sharp edges and leaving a rounded corner.

Some more recent tools of considerable use to boat builders are Surform tools (fig. 3G). These have removable blades with masses of teeth which cut in a way which may be likened to filing. There are plane and file type holders for using the blades flat, but others have blades curved either in the length or width. These are particularly useful in the many shaped parts of a boat. Besides their use on solid wood, they are satisfactory on the crossing grains of the edge of plywood, which does not take kindly to the more traditional spokeshave.

Related to planes are chisels and gouges. Gouges are rarely needed, but a few chisels have their uses. General-purpose chisels are known as firmer chisels and $\frac{1}{4}$ in., $\frac{1}{2}$ in. and $\frac{3}{4}$ in. are suitable sizes to start with if new ones have

to be bought. If a little extra is paid for bevel-edged chisels
they will get into corners as well as do all that the square-
edged chisels will.

A very large number of holes have to be drilled when
building any boat. For holes in wood up to at least $\frac{1}{4}$ in.
the usual bits are Morse pattern twist bits. These are
really metal-working drills, but they are available in sizes
which go in steps of only a few thousandths of an inch, so
drills can be found to suit any screw, nail or bolt. The
most expensive bits are high-speed steel. These tend to be
brittle and are unnecessarily expensive for woodwork.
Carbon steel or jobbers drills are cheaper and better for
woodworking.

A hand-operated wheel-brace is suitable for use with
these bits, although a small hand electric drill will lessen
labour and speed the work. If only one power tool is
bought it should be a drill. For larger holes a carpenter's
brace and bits are needed. Simple centre bits are cheap,
but only really suitable for shallow holes. It is better to
get twist bits. Of the several types, Irwin pattern is a good
one. Ideally a set starting at the size of the largest Morse
pattern drill and going in $\frac{1}{16}$ in. steps up to $\frac{3}{4}$ in. will
be needed, although it is more economical to see what is
needed for the boat chosen and buy bits as needed.
Countersinking in wood or metal is most effectively done
at low speeds and the carpenter's brace is better than a
wheel brace or power drill. The humble bradawl is not
to be despised for making small holes. Gimlets should be
avoided—they enter with a splitting action. A long
pointed spike, such as an ice pick, is useful for marking
through holes or lining them up.

Almost any hammer will do what hitting is necessary,
although for riveting over roves a lighter one than is
customary is better. A 4 oz. hammer with a cross pane is
suitable. The ball pane of an engineer's hammer is more

suitable for heavier riveting. Ideally, chisel handles are hit with a mallet, but a hammer does not harm plastic handles and where wood parts have to be driven together a piece of scrap wood over them allows a hammer to be used.

In some forms of construction a great many screws have to be driven. It is important that screwdrivers should fit the screws. A number of cheap plain screwdrivers to suit the various sizes of screws will be more use than an expensive screwdriver which is only an approximate fit for some screws. Pump-action screwdrivers allow quicker assembly, but they are costly and more than one size may be needed, even allowing for changeable bits. Ratchet screwdrivers come between the plain and the pump type, but they do not seem to have found much favour. The choice of screwdriver is mainly personal preference, but it is the end which fits the screw slot which really matters.

For measuring, the tape-like expanding rule 10 ft. or so long is worth buying, although a steel tape measure will also do the job. In boat building the measurements to be checked are often greater than in other amateur woodworking, and many steps with a short rule may lead to errors. A 24 in. straight steel rule is used as much as a straight-edge as for measuring. A combination square will mark small right angles and it has other uses. Larger right angles are laid out geometrically. Many jobs in boat building involve cutting angles, and an adjustable bevel with a quick-action lock is worth having.

A professional or an expert amateur will frequently sharpen his edge tools. The beginner tends to carry on with a tool which is getting progressively blunter and begrudge any time taken for sharpening. Chisels, plane irons, knives and other cutting tools are easier to use and do better work if sharp. Sharpness is a matter of degree. The two surfaces of a tool should meet at an acute angle which is of no thickness and without ridges. This is impossible to achieve, but we aim to get as near as possible.

Chisels and plane irons usually have two bevels, although thin blades have only one. The long bevel is made on a grindstone (fig. 4A) and the short bevel on an oilstone (fig. 4B). Grinding is best done on a traditional slow-moving sandstone lubricated with water, but today a small high-speed abrasive wheel is more common. The

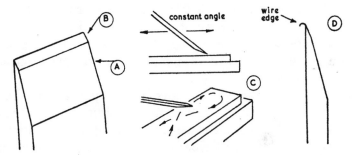

Fig. 4. Tool sharpening

danger with this is overheating. If rainbow colours come when grinding this means that the temper has been drawn and the edge is soft. To prevent this the tool must be frequently dipped in water.

Fortunately the need for grinding is rare, and most sharpening is done on an oilstone. The usual size is about 8 in. × 2 in. × 1 in. and it is possible to get double-sided stones, with coarse and fine grits. The oil used should be thin. A light lubricating oil, or even paraffin, is better than anything as thick as motor oil. Keep the stone clean. A wooden case with a lid is almost essential. To sharpen, try to maintain the same angle, as the edge is rubbed the full length of the stone. If it is a narrow chisel move it about so as to avoid wearing a groove in the stone. The existing bevel will give a clue to the angle (fig. 4C). One hand fairly high on the tool provides control and thrust, while the fingers of the other hand provide the pressure.

Continue rubbing until a 'wire edge' can be felt on the other side when a finger is passed down the surface towards the edge. When the roundness of the blunt edge has been rubbed away and the two surfaces again meet, further rubbing removes a tiny sliver of waste steel, which turns over. This is the 'wire edge' (fig. 4D). To remove it from a chisel or plane iron, rub the other surface absolutely flat on the stone a few times, then slice the blade across the edge of a piece of scrap wood. With a knife, or other tool which has to be sharpened on both sides, continue until the wire edge can be felt, then slice across a piece of wood.

A coarse stone will remove metal quickly, but the resulting edge will be rather like a miniature saw with teeth spaced about the same size as the grit in the stone. Except for coarse work sharpening should be repeated on a fine stone to remove these coarse 'teeth' and replace them with finer ones.

Much finishing work on wood is done by sanding—really an obsolete term. The common abrasive paper is coated with glass, not sand. This is cheapest, but does not last long. The traditional names of grades are: 3, strong 2, middle 2, fine 2, 1½, 1, 0, 00 and even more os; the finer grades also being called 'flour' paper. For general work on a boat 'middle 2' is a suitable paper. A snag with common glasspaper is that the glue holding the particles of glass is not waterproof. Paper which has absorbed moisture will lose all its cut after the first rub. A better abrasive is the synthetic grit bonded to cloth or paper with a waterproof glue and generally described as 'wet and dry paper', as it can be used for rubbing down with a flow of water to keep the surface free of grit and dirt.

Power sanding needs caution. A sanding disc driven by an electric drill can soon leave a surface covered in curved ridges, which are difficult to remove. A drum sander is a better tool. An orbital sanding attachment will give a good finish, but it is a slow worker. The ideal power sander is a belt sander, but this is a costly tool.

Not many metalworking tools are needed, but a hacksaw to take 10 in. blades will do most cutting. A 'Junior' hacksaw to take 6 in. blades is worth having for small work. Files have traditional names. A 10 in. second-cut hand file is a general-purpose tool. Its teeth are a medium size and the sides are parallel. If you ask for a flat file you get one tapered in its width. With this may go a 6 in. half-round second-cut file, and the two will tackle most jobs. If you want a triangular file its name is 'three-square'. The drills already described will suit metal, but one or two centre punches are needed to make dents to locate the position of holes. Fairly large tin snips (say 12 in.) will cut sheet metal.

Pliers and pincers are always useful, but a 'Mole' grip is worth having, as it can lock on to a job, serving as a means of holding small parts, as well as an adjustable spanner. Many boats are built without a vice, but a woodworking vice on a substantial bench makes accurate work, especially prefabricating parts, much easier. A metalworking vice is not so important, but a small one which cramps on the bench or a convenient plank has many uses.

Other tools are described in connection with particular jobs in Chapter 4.

4

BASIC PROCESSES

AT ONE time there was a certain mystique about boat building, with special terms peculiar to the job, which made the whole thing seem more complicated than it was, even to anyone who might already be a good crafts- man in some other trade. Much of this has passed, and drawings and descriptions are usually in everyday language and any technicality will follow that used in general engineering or woodworking.

Drawings of boats intended for amateur construction usually include plenty of pictorial views and actual sizes of parts, which have been worked out by the designer. Frames and shaped parts are often drawn full-size. Tradi- tionally, a designer provided the boat builder with a 'lines drawing' with a 'table of offsets' (fig. 5). From this the boat builder set out the same thing full-size to get the shape of the outside of the boat, then allowed for thick- nesses of planking, the arrangement of stem and other parts which penetrated the skin, and so arrived at the shape of frames or formers. The designer, working to a small scale, might have errors of $\frac{1}{2}$ in. or so on some measurements when drawn full-size and the boat builder had to 'fair the lines' to correct this. This is called 'lofting'. When a large round-bottomed hull is to be built this still has to be done, but for most small craft, especially those

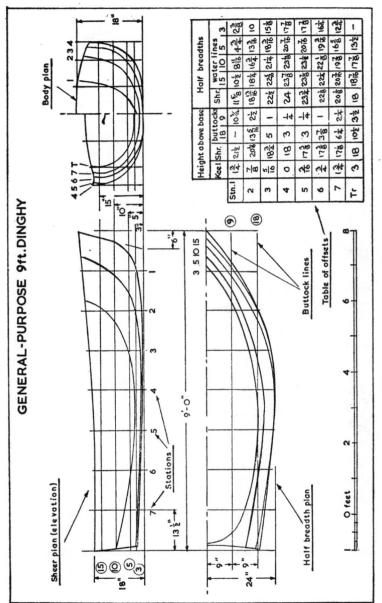

Fig. 5. A typical lines drawing

with plywood skins, none of this preliminary work has to be done by the boat builder. He can start straight away on constructional work.

A lines drawing may not be needed by the builders of most modern small boats, but an understanding of its principles is worth having. The descriptions of larger craft in yachting magazines are often accompanied by these drawings and a practised eye can interpret the shape of the hull from them. A designer has to start with a lines drawing, even if he does not need to pass it on to the builder, because he is able to provide him with all the constructional information in other ways.

There is a view from the side, which most people call an 'elevation', but which may be called a 'sheer plan'. Below it there is a view from above, usually of only half the boat and called a 'half-breadth plan'. To one side is a drawing of several half-sections at various points along the boat. This is a 'body plan'.

To ensure a smooth shape and all of the lines being fair, the designer marks in several horizontal and vertical sections, then draws the shapes of each of these slices. As a further check, he draws diagonal cuts across the body plan and obtains the shapes of these slices. All of this is a tedious business of checking and cross-checking until points on a curve in one direction agree with points on curves in another direction. Vertical cuts are called 'buttock lines'. Horizontal cuts are called 'water lines', although only one may be the actual designed water line, usually called the 'load water line' (L.W.L.).

If a boat is to be built from a lines drawing the first job is to reproduce the drawing full-size on the floor, using the table of off-sets to locate points on the curves from base lines. Curves are then drawn around battens sprung through these points. The shapes of frames and other parts are drawn after allowing for the thickness of the skin.

Building on frames

Most small craft are built upside-down on frames (more correctly called 'formers' if they do not form part of the finished boat). The frames usually have to be fixed to the workshop floor and the only 'lofting' is the marking out of the floor to position the frames, stem and transom. A centre line has the positions of the parts marked on it and lines drawn across at right angles.

Straight lines more than a few feet long are best 'struck' with a chalk line. This is fine string or stout thread (crochet cotton is very suitable) on which chalk is rubbed. One end of the line is held by an assistant or a bradawl. You walk back from this, letting the line unwind as you rub chalk on it. At the other end you stretch the line without jerking it. For a length up to about 12 ft. you can reach towards the middle and lift the line a few inches, then let it spring back to deposit a line of chalk on the floor. If the length is more than this get someone else to 'strike' the line near the centre (fig. 6A).

The commonest method of setting out a large right angle accurately is the '3 : 4 : 5' method. This is based on the fact that in a triangle with sides in those proportions, the angle between the two short sides is a right angle. From the point where the angle is to be, measure four units along the base line, then make an arc of three units from the same point in a position which will obviously contain the right angle (fig. 6B). This can be done with a tape measure and a sharpened piece of chalk held against the distance mark. From the other mark on the base line measure five units to a point on the arc (fig. 6C). Strike a line through this mark and the original mark on the base line. The size of the unit chosen will depend on the size of the layout. Using 2 ft. as a unit gives a furthest mark 6 ft. from the base line. Choose a unit which takes this mark

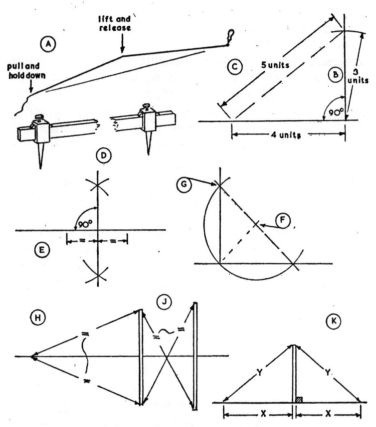

FIG. 6. Methods of setting out

at least as far as the furthest part of the layout is to be. Only one right angle need be marked. All others can be marked parallel to it.

Trammels are useful. These are sliding heads which mount on a strip of wood (fig. 6D). The alternative is to drive nails through a strip of wood. If the base line extends both sides of where the right angle is to come, as when using the position of a middle frame for the basic right angle, the trammels (or wood and nails) can be used.

Measure equal distances each side of the mark for the right-angle crossing. Put the trammels on these in turn and make arcs which cross. A line struck through these crossings will be a right angle (fig. 6E).

For a right angle near the end of a base line the trammels can be used. Put one point where the right angle is to be, and the other anywhere convenient so that trammel beam or strip of wood is about 45 deg. to the base line (fig. 6F). Swing around this point to cross the base line again and to make an arc where the right angle is likely to be. Strike a line through the crossing on the base line and the point which was the centre of the curve. Where the line crosses the arc is a point on a right-angle line (fig. 6G).

Boat building is not precision engineering and there can be quite large tolerances in some things, but it is important that a boat is built straight and reasonably symmetrical. Once an accurate centre line has been established and another line at right angles to it, all other measurements should be based on them. Squareness may be further checked by measuring diagonals, either from a point on the centre line (fig. 6H) or across corners of two frames (fig. 6J).

Frames must stand vertically. A plumb line may be used at the centre of a frame (any weighted string). Distances may be measured each side of the frame along the centre line and diagonal measurements checked to be equal (fig. 6K).

The method of building up frames will be specified on the plan. For a plywood boat the frames are usually made of strips with some sort of gusset at the corners, whether single or double chine. A simple overlap (fig. 7A) or a gusset between the parts (fig. 7B) is unsatisfactory because of difficulty in fairing off tapers to match the skin. This is sometimes used on almost parallel punts. To keep the

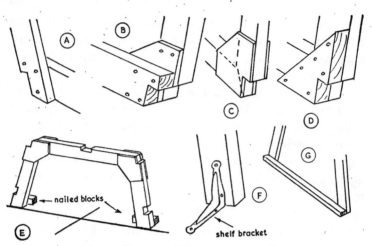

FIG. 7. Frame and former construction

parts in line there may be two plywood gussets (fig. 7c) or one more substantial joint cover (fig. 7d). These last frames are usually set up so that any taper is on the side away from the joint cover, and all frames in a boat may not be the same way round. Bevelling to match the skin is then on the frame parts only and the joint cover may not make contact with the skin.

For a boat intended to be built upside-down on frames, the sides of the frames extend to make feet, which will be cut off afterwards. The feet may be nailed to the floor (fig. 7e) or fixed with angle brackets (fig. 7f). There may be a crossbar at floor level (fig. 7g and plates 6 and 11). This can be nailed after a centre line marked on it has been lined up with the base line on the floor. Transoms are usually made of plywood, framed up and with legs similar to frames. The stem also extends to the floor and is nailed over the centre line.

During building, the strains put on the structure tend to lift the ends, so stem and transom should be particularly well secured to the ground. If the workshop floor is concrete, several stout timbers should be laid lengthways. One may carry the centre line and others should be arranged parallel to it at distances that will suit the fixing of the frame legs or crossbars.

Fastenings

The number of metal fastenings to be driven in most boats necessitates correct technique, especially as it is often necessary to fasten down large areas within the adjusting time specified by the glue makers.

A screw holds parts together by pulling the top piece down by pressure of the head. This means that the hole in the top piece must not be tight—the screw must slide through a clearance hole and not have to be driven into it. The hole in the lower piece must be under-size, so that the screw cuts into it. In hardwood the hole may be slightly bigger than in softwood. It should go almost to the full depth of the screw, but in softer wood the screw may be left to penetrate the last short distance without a hole (fig. 8A). For a countersunk head the hole may have to be prepared with a countersink bit, but the smaller screw heads will pull into many woods and plywood. Countersinking with a bit may then cause them to pull in further than intended. A few experiments will show is countersinking is necessary. Most drilling for screws if done with twist drills, but for some sizes of screws there are combination drills which make both sizes of hole and countersink in one operation (fig. 8B).

In many places the best finish is obtained by counter-boring the hole so that the screw head is below the surface (fig. 8c). This can be covered by a stopping paste, but a wood plug is better. A piece of dowel rod will leave exposed end grain which will show, even under paint. It

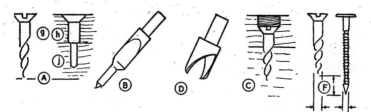

Screw gauge	Actual diam. (g)	Clearing drill (h)	Tapping drill (j) softwood | hardwood	
4	·108"	7/64"	small bradawl hole	
5	·122"	1/8"	"	
6	·136"	9/64"	"	
7	·150"	5/32"	3/32"	3/32"
8	·164"	11/64"	3/32"	3/32"
10	·192"	13/64"	1/8"	1/8"
12	·220"	15/64"	1/8"	1/8"
14	·248"	1/4"	9/64"	5/32"
16	·276"	9/32"	11/64"	3/16"

FIG. 8. Drilling for screws

is better to use plugs with the grain crosswise. They can be bought, but a plug cutter (fig. 8D) to use in a drilling machine will make plugs from offcuts of the wood being plugged, ensuring a good match. The table gives drill sizes for commonly used screws, but variations may have to be made in the tapping size according to the hardness of the wood (fig. 8E).

If barbed ring nails are substituted for screws in a design where only screws are specified they should be slightly longer, but thinner (fig. 8F). In the smallest sizes only flat heads are available, and these will hammer flush. In the larger sizes flat and countersunk heads may be had, and the latter are generally preferable. In the small sizes used for fixing plywood skins on small boats there is no need to drill, except where a nail comes near an edge and there might be a risk of splitting. For quick assembly, and to reduce risk of nails bending, all nails should be driven

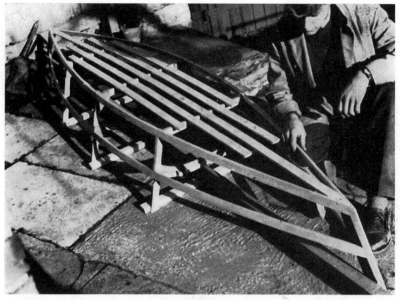

PLATE 6

A typical flat-bottomed framework ready for covering with plywood. This
is a canoe, in which the bottom stringers also serve as bottom boards

The first side panel being fitted to a 9 ft. frameless Curlew sailing dinghy.
Recesses in the formers are bevelled to allow the boat to be lifted off

PLATE 7

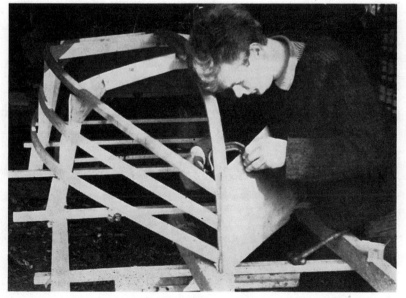

PLATE 8

Above: A bottom panel being fitted to a Curlew dinghy. The change from butt to overlap along the chine may be seen, where the surplus plywood has not yet been planed off. *Below:* The hull of a Curlew dinghy nearing completion. The thwarts hold the boat in shape and support the centreboard case. The breasthook is a grown knee, but the thwart knees are laminated

PLATE 9

until almost through the top piece before bringing the parts together.

Copper nails are not so often used for ordinary nailing, but where they are, holes should be drilled first, otherwise they will bend. The hole should be slightly undersize and drilled to at least half the depth of the nail. These square nails may have flat or countersunk heads and are made in a considerable range of thicknesses and lengths, particularly for riveting parts together in traditional boat building.

The alternative to riveting is to clench nail. The nail is driven through and the point turned over. At one time galvanised steel nails were clenched in cheap construction, but hammering removed the zinc coating, exposing the steel to rust. Entire construction in this way is not recommended, but there are occasions when clenching is desirable—fixing plywood skin joint covers is one example (plate 13). To make up length, the skin panels butt and the joint is covered by a plywood strap glued inside. Copper nails could be used to hold the parts together, but brass nails about 16 or 18 gauge (shoe nails) are neater and stiff enough to drive without drilling (fig. 9A).

Nails are driven from outside, while the inside is supported slightly to one side of the nail being driven. The head of each nail is supported by an iron block, while the

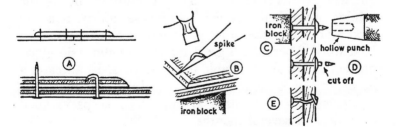

FIG. 9. Nail clenching and riveting

end is hammered over inside. An improvement on bending straight along the grain is to curve the end by hammering over a spike, then bury the point across the grain (fig. 9B).

To rivet with nails and roves, drive a nail through an undersize hole, then support the head with a hammer or iron block. Choose a rove with a hole slightly smaller than the nail and drive it on, preferably with a hollow punch (fig. 9c), although a piece of wood with its end grain against the nail may be used. Cut off the end of the nail about $\frac{1}{16}$ in. above the rove (fig. 9D). With light blows from a light hammer (4 oz. for most nails) spread the end of the nail over the rove. Heavy blows tend to bend the nail in the thickness of the wood (fig. 9E). Later strain on the joint may cause the nail to straighten and the joint to open.

Glued construction

Synthetic resin glues have little in common with the older animal and fish glues. Setting is a chemical action. Once a synthetic resin glue has set, nothing will soften it. These glues set hard and rigid and cannot be used with flexible materials.

Casein glue is derived from milk. It is water-resistant, but will lose its strength in damp conditions. Before the coming of synthetic resins it had its uses afloat. It is still used ashore, but the other glues have taken its place for boat work. There are a great many synthetic resin glues, but not many are available to small users. In all cases a hardener causes the resin to set. Until the resin meets the hardener it remains as a syrup, which keeps in good condition for several months.

One commonly used type (Aerolite) consists of a syrup

which is applied to one surface, and a liquid hardener which is applied to the other surface. The two parts are brought into contact, adjustment must be made within ten minutes, then they are held lightly cramped for a period depending on the temperature and the grade of hardener. If the glue is bought as a syrup it is Aerolite 300, but it may be bought as a powder (Aerolite 306), which will keep for several years. This is mixed with water to make the syrup.

Another commonly used type is Cascamite 'Waterproof'. This appears to be one powder, but is both syrup and hardener in powder form, which do not affect each other dry. Only sufficient is mixed with water for use in an hour or so.

Beetle 'A' is a syrup with which a liquid hardener is mixed before use. The mixture must be used within an hour or a little longer, depending on temperature. This glue is light brown, but the other two are white. Steel will cause staining, with any of the glues, so glue must not be put in steel containers and any brushes should not be mounted in metal. Glass or plastic pots are suitable. A soft plastic pot (cut-off 'squeezee' container) can be flexed to release any glue which hardens in it. Some woods, particularly some varieties of oak, may stain.

There are even stronger glues with increased water resistance, such as Aerodux, and others, such as Araldite, which will make strong joints in many materials, including metals. For normal amateur boat building the types mentioned have more than adequate strength. If an attempt is made to break a joint, the wood fibres break before the glue line gives way.

If wood has to be joined to make up lengths the ends can be tapered and scarfed (also spelled 'scarphed'). The recommended angle of bevel is not less than 1 in 8 (i.e. 4 in. long on $\frac{1}{2}$ in. wood). To plane a bevel without

marking out, one piece is put on top of the other, set
back the correct distance, and the two planed together
(fig. 10A). Cramp the glued parts with paper (to prevent
the pressure pieces sticking) (fig. 10B). Plywood may be
scarfed, but if the width is much (say over 12 in.), it is
difficult to make an accurate job of hand planing. The
edges of plywood may be planed in the same way as solid
wood, but to prevent flexing there should be a stout flat
board under the edge (fig. 10C). Most marine plywood

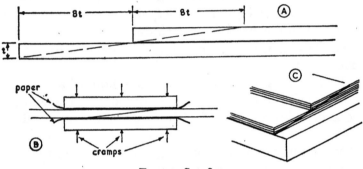

FIG. 10. Scarfing

makers will scarf sheets to order. For most small boat
building a strong joint, if not such a neat one, will result
from using joint covers inside butted panels, rather than
risk a poor scarf on a wide panel.

With synthetic resin glues laminated parts may be built
up from thin strips, giving a stronger and less-wasteful
part than can be made by cutting from a solid block. The
work is simpler, although a mould may have to be made
first.

Most boats have knees—wooden angle brackets
strengthening corners. At one time wood had to be
selected with twisted grain, such as where a branch left
the trunk, so that the grain approximated to the shape
(fig. 11A). A stronger and better-looking knee can be

made with several layers of quite thin wood and a small solid piece in the corner (fig. 11B and plate 9). Clamps pull the pieces into the curve while the glue sets, or the parts may be pulled around a former before fitting to the boat. A cranked tiller, made of strips of wood of contrasting colour, looks attractive and is strong (fig. 11C).

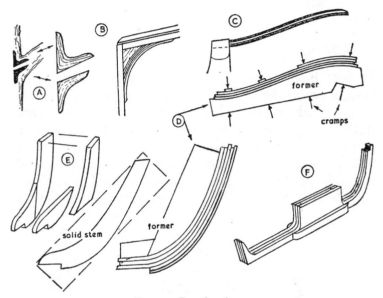

FIG. 11. Laminating

A solid stem may have to be cut from quite a large and costly piece of wood. Laminating is simple (fig. 11D and plate 2). Formers, or moulds can be made from scrap wood. Only the surface against the laminations has to be accurately made.

Sometimes the strength of glue can be used to build up parts in what may be called 'vertical lamination'. Several pieces, cut with the minimum waste, can be built up into what would otherwise be a solid block (fig. 11E). Plywood is sometimes built up in this way—it is possible to make one assembly of stem, hog, centreboard case and stern knee to make a lengthwise girder, having differing thicknesses to suit the local loads and construction (fig. 11F). The only snag with this is that the skin and other parts may have to be glued to the plywood girder edgewise to the ply, and glue does not bond as well to end grain as it does to side grain.

Cramping

In boat building much ingenuity is often called for in holding parts together. Anyone building even a small boat is never likely to find he has too many ordinary G cramps, but there are many places where these cannot be used. Struts from the roof or the walls, or even two or three helpers sitting on a part being fixed, are recognised methods. Folding wedges are a good method of applying considerable pressure (fig. 12A), either to tighten a strut

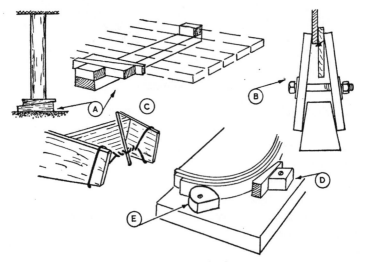

FIG. 12. Improvised cramps

(plate 3) or squeeze between blocks. Two boards lightly bolted may have the ends forced together by a wedge at the other end (fig. 12B). A Spanish windlass can exert a useful pull (fig. 12c and plate 4). For light laminations the former can be on a board, so that pressure can be applied with wedges and blocks screwed on (fig. 12D). Cams may be used (fig. 12E). Fortunately, with synthetic resin glue, great pressure s not needed. Sufficient tightness to hold the parts in contact is better than excessive pressure which may force out too much glue and starve the joint.

Spiling

There are not many straight lines in a boat and the curves which have to be drawn and matched are not always easy to mark. Sometimes a piece may be put directly over the place where it is to fit and the shape pencilled around, or a template may be made from stiff paper, old linoleum or hardboard. This is shaped by trial and error and variations noted before cutting the actual wood which is to fit. This method is often used, but a more craftsmanlike way is to use spiling, which is a method of transferring a shape from the job to the piece which is being fitted, using a distance piece and reference marks on a board.

If a plank has to fit against another curved one, a piece of scrap wood or hardboard is cut very approximately to shape and put into position. A short block of wood is run around with a pencil against its end (fig. 13A). This is transferred to the board which is to be fitted, by putting the scrap board over it and moving the marking block around level with the drawn line, while pencil marks are made at its end (fig. 13B). A variation on this is to use a straight marking board with a straight line drawn on it.

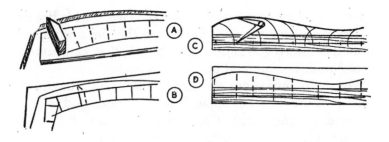

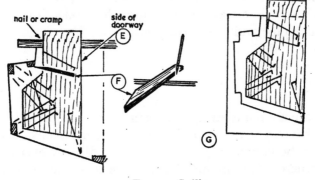

FIG. 13. Spiling

This is cramped in place and distances at several places taken from the centre line with dividers, which are swung round each time to mark the board (fig. 13C). The board is put on the part to be cut and the dividers reset at each point then swung back to about right angles to the board (fig. 13D). A curve is drawn through these marks with a pencil and a springy batten.

If the shape to be copied is more complex, as when getting the shape for a bulkhead, the method is slightly different. Fix a fairly large piece of scrap plywood or hardboard in place. If one edge can be exactly on the centre line of the boat or at the side of a cabin door, that will be a help in transferring the shape without waste (fig. 13E). Have a pointed stick and put its sharp end against key points in turn, then draw around its end on the main board (fig. 13F). For curves, do this at several points. Remove this pattern and put it on top of the plywood for the bulkhead. Put the pointed stick back into its marked positions and mark where the point comes. Join up these points (fig. 13G).

Steaming

In traditional boat building much use was made of steaming. A piece of wood will bend easier if soaked in steam for some time, and for large craft this is the only way of making the comparatively large-sectioned wood sufficiently pliable. However, laminating has taken the place of much bending of stouter wood which needed steaming, and for most small craft there is no need to steam. A snag with steaming in modern construction is that synthetic resin glues cannot be used with wet wood. This means that a steamed part has to be bent to shape and fixed there temporarily to dry out completely, then it is removed and glue applied.

If steaming is necessary a steaming box has to be rigged. This is something large enough to contain the parts to be steamed, with plenty of space around them for steam to circulate. In its most elementary form this is a piece of rainwater pipe and a kettle with a hose attached to the spout. The ends are plugged with rags (fig. 14A). In a larger size, the box is built up from wood and water is boiled in an oil drum with a hose to carry the steam (fig. 14B).

In a small boat the parts which need most bending are usually the chines. It is always the best policy to bend the parts of greatest curvature first. With chines, this is the part near the stem. Fix both chines to the stem and pull in both together. If they will not go fully into place, pull

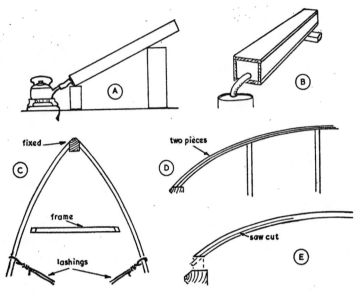

FIG. 14. Steaming and bending

as far as you dare and lash the aft ends down (fig. 14C). If this can be left overnight the wood will probably go the rest of the way next day without further treatment. If not, rags wrapped around the wood and soaked with hot water will help. Steam from an electric kettle played on the part resisting bending is also useful.

The alternative is to laminate the chines with two pieces of half thickness, pulled into place with synthetic resin glue between, and fixed down while the glue is still liquid, working back from the stem (fig. 14D). A variation on this is to use a solid strip, but run a fine circular saw along its centre for at least as far as the greater curve will extend, leaving the aft straighter part uncut (fig. 14E). Without glue this is bent around and cramped in place temporarily, starting from the aft end, and the stem end cut. It is removed and the saw kerf sprung open for glue to be applied, then it is fixed permanently.

5

CLINKER CONSTRUCTION

DATING back at least to Viking and Egyptian days, clinker planking is still an accepted method of planking boats, although because of the special skill needed, it is not as commonly employed today; but when used by experienced craftsmen it is one of the quickest ways of building a small boat. For an amateur it provides an interesting job, which gives a lot of satisfaction and the result is what most people mean when they say they want 'a boat which looks like a boat'.

Planks are laid fore and aft, with the upper plank overlapping the edge of the one below (fig. 15). In conventional clinker construction there are bent ribs or frames inside around the hull, and everything is held together with rivets made with copper nails and roves, through the plank overlaps and through the ribs. A large number of narrow planks gives a more rounded hull than when there are fewer wide ones.

Some high-speed power boats have been built with reverse clinker planking—the lower planks overlapping the ones above. This may be expected to give slightly better lift, but the method is rarely seen today.

A modern version of clinker planking is used in some racing sailing dinghies, where the planking is made of plywood and the lands (overlaps) are glued with synthetic resin, without ribs or metal fastenings. This makes a tight and light hull, but the only satisfactory way of doing this is to have special strip heating to quickly set each glued joint, and this equipment is unlikely to be available to an amateur.

The simplest clinker-planked boat to build is a pram dinghy. Finishing planking on a bow board or transom is easier than at a stem. The boat is built upside-down and

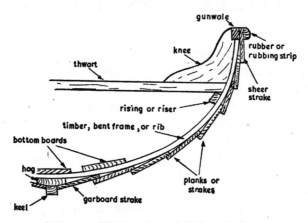

FIG. 15. Half-section of clinker dinghy

for lengths up to about 8 ft. there is only one former, located near the middle of the boat. This, with the shaped bow board and transom, provides sufficient guide and support for the planks as they are laid.

A plan will give the shapes of the former and the two ends, either as a lines drawing on which the thickness of planking must be allowed for, or as full-size drawings of each part. Sometimes the end shapes are given perpendicular to the building line (fig. 16A). As the transom is usually almost vertical, its shape will only be slightly different from the perpendicular one, but on many prams, so as to keep the bow board above the water and at an angle that will throw back waves, it is at a considerable angle to the vertical (fig. 16B). To get its shape from a perpendicular section, draw half of the latter section full-size. From this project a side view of it. Divide the perpendicular section into any number of parts, continued

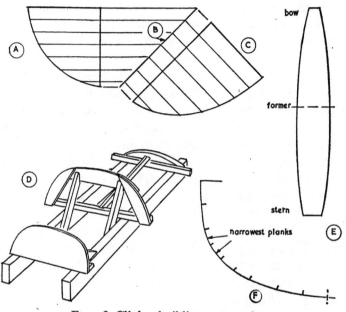

FIG. 16. Clinker-building preparations

to the bow-board view, where they are projected at right angles to it. Measure the half-widths on the perpendicular section and mark them on the same projected lines. A curve through these points will give the shape of the bow board (fig. 16C).

Make the former of scrap wood, but it should be fairly stout as at some stages in building it has to take a considerable thrust. Transom and bow board are usually made of solid wood. Mahogany, oak and elm are suitable.

The parts may be set up on one broad or two narrow stiff planks, which are fixed to trestles on the ground. Alternatively, there may be legs attached to the parts, and these are fixed to the workshop floor. What will later be the upper edges of transom and bow board are usually left straight for fixing down, and shaping is left until the boat is turned over. Some preliminary bevelling of the ends can be done, using the drawing as a guide, but there will have to be some touching up of angles as planking proceeds. Set up the parts at the correct angles and square to the centre line. Brackets can be used, supplemented by struts if necessary (fig. 16D). Planking is done from the centre outwards, so a temporary lath can be fixed around the gunwale line to help hold the parts in position, if desired.

Varnished mahogany always makes an attractive small clinker dinghy, but spruce is often used for lightness and many woods which are free from loose knots are suitable. Traditionally, clinker boats were built with dry joints. Close fits and swelling of the wood in water gave waterproofness. Nowadays it is worth while using synthetic resin glue in all joints. Planking for this type of boat is usually no more than ⅜ in. thick.

In a pram dinghy there is no central hog and keel. Instead, building starts with a wide plank. Its shape may be specified on the plan, but because of the bulbous shape being covered, all planks are wider at the centre and narrower on the bow board than at the transom. A probable shape is shown (fig. 16E). The curves are drawn around a lath sprung to shape. The plank is cut a little too long, so that it overlaps both ends.

The width of other planks depends on the available wood and the number of planks each side. Plank widths need not all be the same. For the greater curvature at the turn of the bilge, the planks may be narrower than at the flatter curves of the bottom and sides (fig. 16F). Measure

around from centre plank to the gunwale line and divide
by the number of planks. Add about ¾ in. for overlaps.
This gives the average widths at the three positions. If the
wood will allow it, the first one or two planks each side
may be more than this, to allow for narrower ones at the
greater curves.

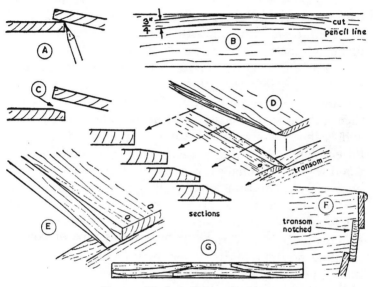

FIG. 17. Fitting clinker planking

Fix the centre plank in position at the ends. Do not have
any fastenings to the central former. Use glue, with screws
or nails into the ends. It is usually possible to mark the
actual planks in position, but templates can be made from
hardboard or card if preferred. Put the wood from which
one of the next planks is to be cut into position, with at
least ¾ in. overlap. Pencil around from below (fig. 17A).
Remove the board and draw a line ¾ in. from this
(fig. 17B). Cut to this line. Mark the widths in the three
positions and draw a curve through the points with a

lath. Cut this edge. Use this plank as a template for its partner at the other side.

Two things have to be done before fitting each plank. The lower plank has to be bevelled so that the other makes a reasonable fit (fig. 17C) and at the ends the upper plank has to be brought to the level of the other. There are two possible ways of doing this. From about 10 in. back from the end plane a twisting bevel for the width of the overlap on both planks (fig. 17D). A neater way is to plane a rebate about 10 in. long on the lower plank (fig. 17E). The upper plank needs no treatment and merely drops into the rebate. Sometimes the rebate in the lower plank is not taken to the full depth at the end, then a shallow rebate is planed in the other plank. This avoids the possibly weak feather edge at the end of the lower plank, but with synthetic resin glue bonding the wood together strongly this extra work does not seem to be justified. On some racing dinghies the transom is notched and the planks are not brought to the same level (fig. 17F), but this calls for some careful workmanship.

Nails along the overlaps have to be spaced to suit the eventual positions of ribs. There may be one or two nails between rib positions. Mark the rib positions on the centre plank. With the help of a mate, put glue on the joint, locate the upper plank and fix with nails near the centre of the boat at positions which will come between ribs. Each nail is driven through a drilled hole and riveted over a rove inside the boat (figs. 9C, D, E). With the plank located at one or two points with nails, fasten down the ends and complete riveting, omitting the places where the nails will come through ribs.

Do the same with the matching plank at the other side. Continue in this way fixing pairs of planks. After a few have been fitted each side, measure the remaining widths to be filled and divide again. Some of the planks may have considerable curve and may not cut very economically from short planks, but long wide boards may cut with curves fitting into each other (fig. 17G). The top plank ('sheer strake') looks best if its edge ('sheer') sweeps up slightly towards the ends when the boat is right way up. A reverse sheer, with the centre higher than the ends is ugly.

The ribs (timbers or bent frames) in a small dinghy are usually made of ash or rock elm in quite thin sections, which bend easily without steaming. Some prebending of the strips helps.

At this stage the boat is turned the right way up, without removing the mould, and leaving the lengthwise base pieces attached, if possible. Start near the middle of the boat and spring a rib into place. Force it down from each side and cramp to the sheer strakes. Drill and rivet through every crossing, starting from the centre plank and working outwards (fig. 18A). Towards the ends it is permissible for the ribs to slope slightly towards the centre of the boat so that they are more nearly at right angles to the skin (plate 5). Fix a temporary strut across the sheer strakes (fig. 18B) and remove the mould and lengthwise base pieces. Leave this strut in place until the centre thwart has been fitted.

The risers, which support the thwarts, are fixed inside the ribs (fig. 18c). The gunwales may be fixed inside the ribs (fig. 18D) or the ribs can be cut back and the gunwales fixed to the sheer strake (fig. 18E). Knees may be fixed to the sheer strake and the gunwales notched in (fig. 18F) or a packing put behind the gunwale (sometimes called an 'inwale' in this case), and longer rivets put through (fig. 18G). Packings are also needed at the rowlock positions (fig. 18H). It is usual to put large knees between the centre plank and the end boards, usually with a ring bolt passed through (fig. 18J) at the bow.

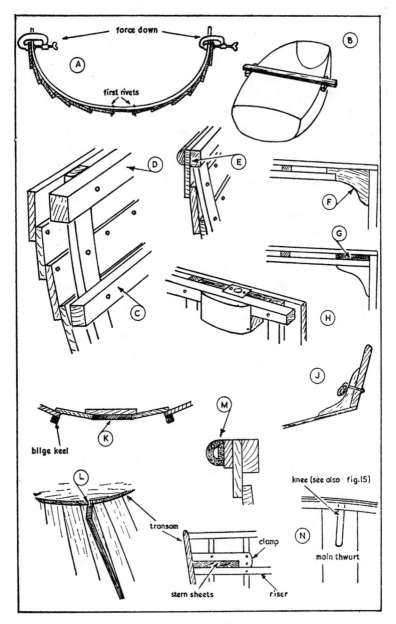

FIG. 18. Fitting out a clinker dinghy

Outside the centre space may be filled (fig. 18K). A skeg aft helps in keeping the boat straight when rowing (fig. 18L). Bilge keels or rubbing strips can be riveted through the second or third overlap out from the centre. The best gunwale rubbing strip is an all-round rubber buffer, mounted on a flat strip (fig. 18M).

Bottom boards are most important and they should be arranged to cover all parts where feet are likely to be put. Offcuts from planking may sometimes be used up, but the arrangement should be sufficiently flexible to pull to the curve of the boat and be held down with turn-buttons, so that the boards are secure in use and can be removed for cleaning.

Thwarts and stern sheets are fixed down to the risers. There may be clamps above them, but at the centre thwart there would be knees, fitted to the gunwales (fig. 18N).

To complete the boat, plank ends are finished flush, tightness of all rivets checked, and everything sanded ready for paint or varnish.

Clinker-planked stem dinghy

In general the building of a stem dinghy is similar to a pram. Apart from the difference in shape there are two main structural differences. Instead of the central plank there is a hog and keel assembly, and at the stem the planks fit into a rebate instead of overlapping, as at the transom.

At one time the keel was notched for the planking, but with synthetic resin glue construction, it is as strong to make the land for the plank (garboard strake) by fixing the keel to the hog (fig. 19A). The stem may be cut from solid wood, with a rebate worked with saw and chisel

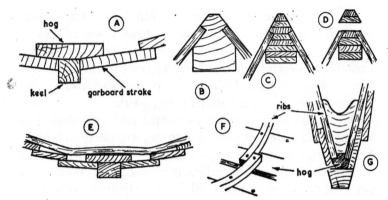

FIG. 19. Details of a clinker stem dinghy

(fig. 19B). It may be easier to make a laminated stem, as the rebate can be made by varying the width of the laminations (fig. 19C). Even easier, only the part which will be inside the rebate is laminated, then the boat planked and the laminations to cover the plank ends applied in position after the plank ends have been trimmed off (fig. 19D).

Depending on the size of the boat, there may be several formers to set up as well as the transom and stem. The design usually calls for the stem and hog to be notched together. Some bevelling of the hog before assembly will reduce the amount of more awkward planing to be done during assembly. The forward end of the hog has to match up with the rebate in the stem, so that the twisted garboard strake drops into a properly faired rebate.

It is fitting the garboard strake which calls for most skill and care. Spiling from a loosely fitting hardboard template is the best way of getting the shape. If some excess length is left at the aft end there will be a little tolerance if fitting is not correct the first time at the stem, and more wood has to be removed. Because of the bevels involved, it may be advisable on a first attempt to make a dummy piece for the forward 2 ft. or so as an experiment. Mark the plank for the opposite side from the first before fitting it.

Bed the garboard strake in glue. Start fixing at the stem end. Cramps will be needed to maintain the twist until all nails or screws are driven into the stem and the forward part of the hog. With the garboard strake fitted, further planking is marked out and fitted in the same way as for the pram dinghy.

From about amidships to the stern, ribs may be continuous from gunwale to gunwale and arched over the hog (fig. 19E). Nearer the stem, the curve at the bottom would be too much for the wood to take. It may be possible to make a rib in two pieces with the ends either meeting or overlapping (fig. 19F). Closer to the stem, the rib ends may notch into the hog, possibly with a floor knee built in (fig. 19G).

Most clinker boats are planked upside-down. Fewer large craft have clinker planking, but when a large boat is to be built by this method it may be planked the right way up, with struts from above holding the formers and other parts on the keel which is supported from below.

6

CARVEL CONSTRUCTION

A CARVEL-PLANKED BOAT has the skin made of strakes laid lengthways, but edge to edge instead of overlapped in the clinker manner. This gives a smooth exterior. The method is not so suitable for thin planking. There is not the support given by the double thickness of the joints in clinker work, so more internal structure is needed. The edge joints have to be made waterproof. Traditionally this was done by caulking, but synthetic resin glues may be used. Caulking is difficult to apply successfully to thin planking. Movement of the boat causing slight flexing of its parts may make the caulking work out. It is unusual for a small boat to be built with carvel planking, but when it is the result is usually a beautiful example of boat-building skill. Moulded veneer construction (see Chapter 8) is a modern method of building a stronger and more watertight boat with a similarly smooth exterior. Carvel planking today is usually at least ⅝ in. thick, and this is used on yachts of at least two tons and more than 24 ft. long.

Caulking

The edges of planks to be caulked are planed to fit tightly on their inner edges, but are bevelled slightly on the outside (fig. 20A). The groove for caulking goes about three-quarters of the way through on thin planking and rather less on thicker wood. The inside of the groove should be painted and the paint allowed to dry before caulking. Traditional caulking consists of strands of cotton covered by a stopping. For large craft oakum is used instead of cotton. This is cheap hemp. Caulking cotton is supplied in balls as a loosely laid rope of eight strands. Only two

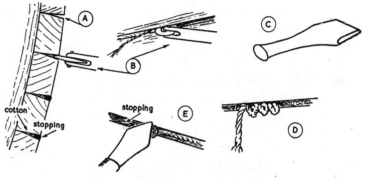

FIG. 20. Caulking carvel planking

or three strands will be needed for seams of smaller yachts. These are twisted together and pressed into the seam. A caulking wheel is used on small seams (fig. 20B). This is followed by a caulking iron (fig. 20C), used with a mallet. The object is to press the cotton very tightly into the seam. The skill comes in driving evenly and sufficiently. Uneven caulking can distort the planking.

For small seams the cotton is merely laid along the groove and driven in. For larger seams it is looped, so as to give a greater bulk, as it is driven (fig. 20D). Cotton is filled into the groove to within about $\frac{1}{8}$ in. of the surface. This is covered with a stopping.

Traditional boat builders have their own recipes for stoppings, but most marine paint makers list a suitable stopping. This stopping or putty must never harden completely as it has to allow for the slight expansion and contraction of the wood. If the seam is painted again after driving the cotton this will give most stoppings a better grip. The stopping is pressed in with a putty knife (fig. 20E) and left to dry off before cleaning off the outside of the hull.

Modern materials have largely superseded traditional caulking materials. There are fibrous caulking compounds, which contain a mineral fibre in a plastic stopping, which can be used for underwater seams without cotton. There are two-part compounds, which make a type of synthetic rubber. The two parts are mixed before use and the paste applied to the seams. Decks, consisting of planks laid lengthways, are often caulked in the same way as carvel planking, but as the seams are on a horizontal surface it is possible to use a stopping material which can be poured. Marine glue is commonly used. This is not a glue in the ordinary sense, but is a flexible stopping which is poured as a hot liquid.

Planking

A carvel-built boat is usually planked on sawn frames, i.e. frames built up from solid wood, although there may be some intermediate bent timbers or ribs. Planking may be shaped in a very similar way to clinker planking, with the greatest width of plank at the point of greatest girth, tapering off towards the ends. However, as the flush planking does not finish with prominent lines at the joints, and planking laid to suit the wood available rather than to obtain a symmetrical appearance does not mar the appearance, it is more usual to keep many of the strips parallel.

This can be done by using narrow strips which permit a certain amount of spring. A wider-shaped piece can be used to correct the run of planking when the need to spring gets too much. A more economical way is to add a short piece, usually triangular, called a 'stealer' (fig. 21A).

To cover a framework with carvel planking start at the garboards and fit the planks there after spiling to get the

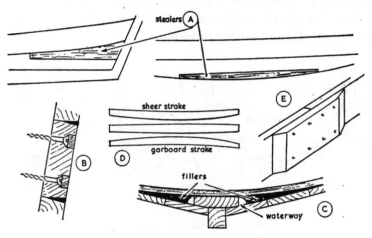

FIG. 21. Carvel-planking details

shape. In a yacht with a stern post there may be considerable twist in this plank aft and steaming may be necessary. Also, to get a sufficient width on the stern post and a good shape to the next plank, a stealer may be needed. One or two more planks may be laid each side against the garboards. Fixing is often by screwing, with the heads counterbored and plugged later (fig. 21B), although copper nails and roves may be used, with the heads sunk and plugged or covered with stopping. If bent timbers are used, fillers should be used where they spring over the hog (fig. 21C).

It is usual to make the sheer strake next and work

downwards from there. Where the curve is greatest, around the turn of the bilge, the planks are almost straight, except for the taper due to the bulbous shape of the hull, while sheer planks are cut with an upward curve and those near the garboard turn downwards (fig. 21D). Where the curve in the girth of the boat is greatest flat planks do not approximate very well to the shape, so it is usual to have narrower planks around the turn of the bilge than above and below it. In large craft some planks may be hollowed on the inside.

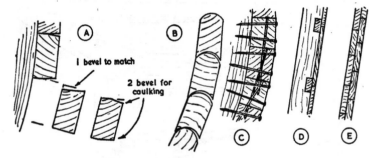

FIG. 22. Special carvel planking

Cutting the necessary curve in a long plank can be very wasteful, so it is usual to make up the length with two or more pieces butted together. It may be possible to join on a wide frame, but a joint cover inside (fig. 21E) is more usual and this is less likely to cause a bump in the fore-and-aft curve of the strake. Of course, butt joints in adjoining strakes should be staggered as much as possible. After planking and caulking, the whole exterior is cleaned off to a smooth curve by planing and sanding.

If strips are used they should not be much wider than they are thick—say 1⅜ in. × 1 in. They may be machine-planed parallel, then hand planed each time to match the one already laid (fig. 22A). It is also possible to have the edges spindled to give meeting curves (fig. 22B). With this sort of planking glued edges are more common than caulked ones. Besides nails or screws to the frames, each plank is nailed, as well as glued, to its neighbour, with nails long enough to pass through it and penetrate a second strip (fig. 22c). Spindled curves do not fit closely for the entire length of the compound curve of a boat, so some stopping may be necessary to get a good finish.

The common phenolic synthetic resin glues do not have very good gap-filling properties, but the more expensive resorcinol glue can be used with a filler, which will take care of most of the openings which occur in this sort of work.

At one time, before the introduction of marine-grade plywood, many small hard-chine boats were covered by seam-batten-carvel planking. This still has its uses. Wide boards which would be too thin for caulking are used and the joints covered inside with battens, glued and either screwed or nailed on (fig. 22D). The battens are let into notches in the framing, then the planks made to meet on their centres.

Occasionally hulls are planked with double carvel strips. The total thickness is made up with planks only half the thickness and they are laid so that joints are staggered (fig. 22E). The thinner pieces of wood are more easily handled and bent, but the amount of work is increased. At one time painted cloth was put between the two skins, but today it would be better to use synthetic resin glue. This makes a strong and waterproof hull, with a resemblance to moulded veneer (see Chapter 8), which is a lighter and more economical way of taking advantage of the properties of modern glues.

7

PLYWOOD BOATS

Most amateur-built boats and many professionally built boats have plywood skins. The combination of large sheets of plywood of uniform quality and fully waterproof glues makes possible the building of boats without a great deal of skill. For a beginner this is the method to adopt. The need for shapes to include curves in one direction only means that sections are angular, but by choosing a good design the lines may still be seaworthy and pleasing.

It is advisable to cover exposed edges of plywood, as water creeping into the end grain may cause staining or rot in the inner veneers. If water has soaked into the wood and the boat is stored in freezing conditions, the water will expand in the plywood as it freezes, causing splitting of the fibres. It is usual to arrange for edges to be covered with solid wood bedded in glue. There may be a rebate (fig. 23A) or two meeting sheets may be bevelled and covered with a half-round moulding (fig. 23B). It is more usual for one panel to overlap the other and for its edge to be covered by a rubbing strip (fig. 23C). At the transom it is customary to merely rely on paint or varnish to seal the edge of the plywood (fig. 23D). The gunwale of a small open boat may also have the ply exposed (fig. 23E), but if there is any decking, the deck covers the side plywood and is itself covered by a rubbing strip (fig. 23F).

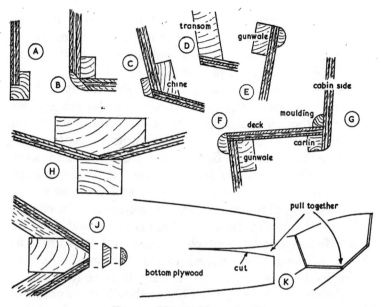

FIG. 23. Plywood-boat details

The inner edge of decking has the plywood covered by a coaming or cabin side (fig. 23G). Other details of a good plywood design are arranged so that as far as possible edges are covered. At the bottom, plywood panels may meet on the hog, then a keel is bedded in glue (fig. 23H). At the stem the plywood may be allowed to overlap during fitting, then after planing off a capping is glued and nailed on (fig. 23J).

Flat-bottomed boat

The simplest hull to cover is one with a flat bottom meeting the sides at a fairly constant angle. This may be a pram type, have a stem and transom, or be double-ended with a pointed stern like a dory or canoe. A variation on this which gives some shape to the bottom is to split the end of the plywood panel so that it can be sprung into a V shape, as in the author's well-known Gremlin and Goblin dinghies (fig. 23K and plate 4).

Some of these boats are built the right way up without frames, but the majority are built over frames upside-down, although the frames (then more correctly called 'formers') may not form part of the finished boat.

For a flat-bottomed boat with a stem and the frames built in, the design usually allows for the frames to have legs to the workshop floor (plate 6) and the transom to be framed-up plywood with legs. The stem may be curved slightly or straight. Plywood which is flat or only slightly curved does not have much stiffness and it is usual to build in lengthwise strips, called 'stringers'. As the stringers have no difficult bending it is convenient to build them in early in assembly as they help to hold the frames squarely in position (fig. 24A). The hog also drops into slots in the frames and may be screwed to the bottom of the stem (fig. 24B).

Bend a gunwale around so as to overlap the stem and mark the angle (fig. 24C). Cut this and try it in position. The notch for it on the first frame will probably have to be bevelled. For ease in fairing off later, arrange any lengthwise parts which fit into notches so that any level-ling off will have to be done to the frame and not the lengthwise part (fig. 24D). Deepen notches if necessary. Prepare both gunwales, but leave them overlong. Fix both to the stem with glue and screws, then pull them back around the frames. If there is any difficulty, see Chapter 4 for ideas to help bending. Put glue in the notches and screw each joint in turn, working aft from frame 1. Cut the transom end to length and fix that.

Treat the chines in the same way, except see that at each frame the wood is only sunk deep enough to allow for fairing off the chine for the bottom (fig. 24E). For the sake of your plane irons, make sure that all screw heads have pulled below the surface.

Fairing off is the most important part of building a

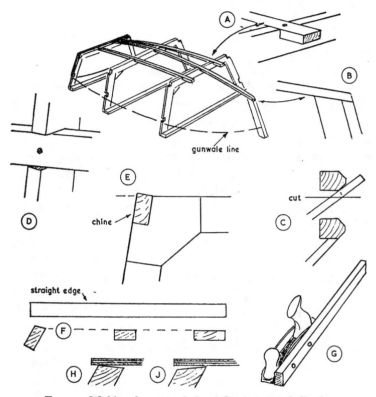

gunwale line

chine

straight edge

cut

FIG. 24. Making framework for a flat-bottomed dinghy

plywood boat. This is preparing all surfaces which will be in contact with the plywood so that there are no bumps or hollows and the skin will make a good contact for glueing with the framing.

Use a long straight edge to test across the framing (fig. 24F) and plane off high spots. If the plane is long enough to bridge gaps that will be a help in ensuring accuracy. A Surform tool with an extending strip of wood is also useful (fig. 24G). Beside the straight edge use a section of plywood to bend over parts of the structure. Be particularly careful at the transom and stem. Although perfection should be aimed at, an error which leaves the joint open slightly inside (fig. 24H) is less trouble than one which is very slightly open outside (fig 24J).

A design for this type of boat usually calls for the sides to be fixed before the bottom. Make a paper template of the side if necessary, although with a small boat it is usually possible to bend the actual plywood sheet. Cramp it around the gunwale and anywhere else possible. Have an assistant press it into place. On the inside, pencil around everything that touches the plywood. Remove the sheet and cut it out with a little to spare. Try it on the opposite side, then use it as a template for marking the other side.

If the panel is to be screwed, drill screw holes within the guide lines. For a dinghy the spacing may be about 3 in. around the edges and 4 in. or more over stringers and frames. Where there is much curve screws may be closer. If the panel is to be fixed with nails, drill through at a few key points to indicate the line of nails on the other side. Drive all nails a short distance.

Apply glue to the frame (and hardener to the plywood if it is a two-part glue). Put the panel in position, with cramps everywhere that it tends to spring, then drive fastenings at a few widely spaced points, particularly at points of greatest strain, then intermediately until all are in. If there is any tendency to spring or buckle it is better to fasten from near the centre of the sheet outwards (fig. 25A). Get both sides on during one session if possible, so as not to leave the framework under unequal strain.

If the boat is too long to be covered with one piece of

PLATE 10

The completed Curlew dinghy, with a gunter mainsail and grooved spars

The double-chine hull for a 16 ft. Nomad cruiser immediately after turning over. The next step is to brace the gunwales and cut off the extensions of the frames

A small plywood pram dinghy nearing completion. The transom has a sculling notch and is stiffened for a small outboard motor

Interior work on a Goblin dinghy. The dagger board trunk is fitted against the thwart. Skin joint covers may be seen on the side near the deck beam and in the bottom near the transom. The framing for a side bench, which will also be a buoyancy compartment, is being made

plywood the length may be made up by scarfing (fig. 25B and plate 10) or by using a joint cover inside (fig. 25C). This can be done after the first panel has been fitted, by fixed pieces between the lengthwise parts (fig. 25D).

When the glue holding the sides has set, fair off the plywood at the ends and along the chines, then fix the bottom in the same way, allowing a little surplus all

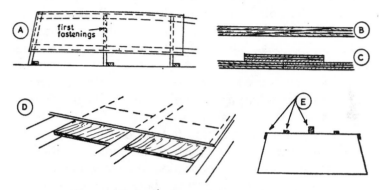

FIG. 25. Fitting a plywood skin on a flat hull

round, to be trimmed off after the glue has set. Any outside pieces on the bottom may be fixed, as well as the rubbing strips around the chines (fig. 25E). To prevent the wood absorbing dirt when the boat is turned over, particularly if it is heavy, it may be advisable to give the bottom one coat of paint or varnish at this stage.

Disconnect the boat from the floor and turn it over. Put a temporary strut across the gunwales near the middle and cut off the extensions of frames, transom and stem. Add risers and any other internal fittings. Leave the strut across until the centre thwart or other stiffening framing is fixed.

Single-chine V-bottom boat

Most plywood boats have a V bottom. This is slightly more difficult to build, but it is more seaworthy and easily driven. The framework is set up in the same way as for a flat-bottomed boat (plate* 7). As there will be a joint along the hog, this is a more substantial piece of wood and the curved stem is usually notched to it (fig. 26A). Towards the stem the bottom panel of plywood will be found to take up a curve in its width. There is still a straight line, but it is diagonal, due to the twist in the panel. This means that when testing for fairing off, the bevels on lengthwise parts towards the stem are not straight across, but curved. Bending a scrap piece of hardboard or thin plywood will show the shape (fig. 26B).

Covering is similar to the flat-bottomed boat, except for the meeting of the two parts of the bottom on the hog (fig. 26c) and a change of section along the chines. For the greater part of the length the bottom panel can overlap the side panel, but near the stem the angle gets increasingly wider until on the stem the bottom and side panels are in line, so that an overlap is impossible. This has to be taken care of by changing from an overlap to a butt joint, at a distance from the stem depending on the design, but probably 12 in. to 24 in. After the side panels have been fixed the aft part of the plywood at the chine is faired off level with the chine (fig. 26D), but forward of the point of change the wood is trimmed to make a mitre with the bottom panel (fig. 26E). This means careful work with a chisel as the bevel varies, bisecting the angle between side and bottom until it is a right angle at the stem.

When a bottom panel is marked out, get the approximate shape at the chine, then notch to fit the side panel and plane and chisel to fit the mitre. This will leave

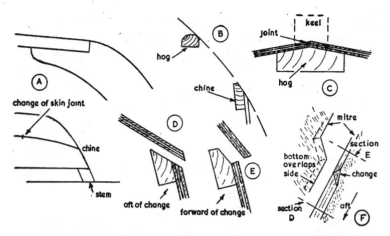

FIG. 26. Fitting a plywood skin on a single-chine V-bottom hull

surplus projecting over the chine aft of this (fig. 26F and plate 8). Bend the panel into place and check that it is correctly along the centre of the hog. Mark the second side from the first. When fixing, start at the mitred joint and work back from it. Let the panel fall naturally into place. Do not distort it. If the edge goes over the centre of the hog, it can be trued with a rebate plane.

Double-chine boat

The single-chine hull has a sharp angle and may look boxlike. Although it gives high speeds under power it is not as seaworthy as a rounded bottom. Many plywood hulls are given a shape nearer the round bottom by having a double chine. This involves a little more work, but the problem of the change of section, which many amateurs find awkward, is avoided.

The hull is built upside-down in the usual way (plate 11). A centreline is marked along each chine and fairing off is done so as to come to this (fig. 27A). So that it may be seen easily, this may be a fairly deep gauge scratch. When marking panels for cutting, edges of the chine piece can

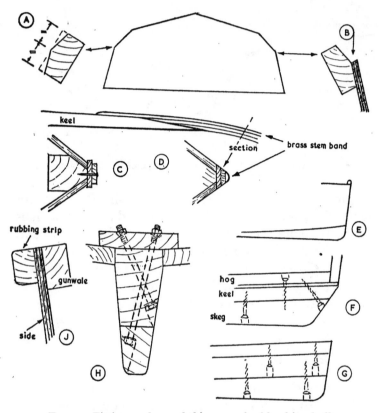

FIG. 27. Fitting a plywood skin on a double-chine hull

be marked, then an extra width allowed to reach the centre. Starting with the side panels, the plywood is fixed and the edges on the chine planed to a mitre with a rebate plane (fig. 27B).

The narrow chine panel is marked to approximate

shape and its meeting edge planed to match the side
panel. Final fitting is by trial and error. When this edge
fits, put the panel in position and mark the other edge.
Fix the chine panel and prepare its edge to meet the
bottom panel. Mark out and fit the bottom panels in the
same way. Other details are the same as for the earlier
boats.

Finishing plywood hulls

The plan used will specify how the stem is to be finished,
but usually the forward end of the keel is planed to a long
bevel and laminated strips are scarfed to it. These pieces
can be slightly too wide and bedded in glue, with nails
driven centrally (fig. 27c). After the glue has set they can
be faired off neatly and probably covered with a half-
round brass strip taken a short distance along the keel
(fig. 27d).

The keel may finish in a skeg aft. With a small boat this
is a help in keeping the boat straight when rowing, it also
helps in steering with an outboard motor. It is not required or desirable on most sailing boats. In the smallest
boat the skeg and keel may be cut from one piece (fig. 27e).
In slightly larger boats it may be a shaped piece fixed with
wood screws which are deeply counterbored (fig. 27f),
from inside and outside. On large craft a point may be
reached where this is impracticable. It may be built up
of several thicknesses, each separately fixed (fig. 27g). It
may be possible to take bolts right through, either straight
or diagonally (fig. 27h).

Decking may be fitted (Chapter 10), but with an open
boat it is advisable to make a strong gunwale, as this often
has to take considerable shocks. A rubbing strip outside
may be almost as thick as the gunwale (or inwale) inside

(fig. 27J). For the same reason, knees should be at least as strong as specified for the clinker boats.

Frameless construction

Any plywood boat may be finished without frames if there is sufficient other internal structure to give the boat rigidity and prevent distortion. In the case of a little pram

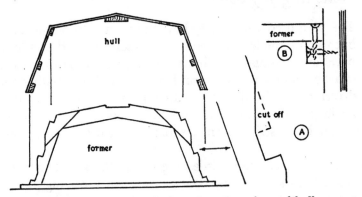

FIG. 28. Former details for a frameless plywood hull

dinghy the central thwart is probably all that is needed to hold the boat in shape. In a larger boat, side decks and buoyancy compartments stiffen the boat (plate 13). Anything that is built in helps.

A frameless boat may be built upside-down in the usual way, but formers have to be made so that the hull will lift off. This means that notches will have to be cut away (fig. 28A and plate 7) and nothing left in which will prevent removal. If there is not much flare to the sides it may be impossible to adapt some designs, as clearance from one part may cut through the notch for another part.

The hog has to be fixed permanently to stem and

transom, but it will probably spring off the formers. One temporary central screw into each is permissible, but plywood panels should be notched around them so that they can be withdrawn after the glue has set on the plywood and before fixing the keel. At the chines screws should be avoided if possible. Cramps may be used, or even string. If there is still a persistent spring away after the side plywood has been tried, a block may be screwed from inside (fig. 28B) and released when the hull is lifted off. Of course, no skin fastenings are made to the formers. It is also important to either fit one or more temporary struts across the gunwales before removing from the formers, or to measure across and pull the hull to these measurements and fix the struts immediately after removal from the formers. From this point the work is the same as for a boat with frames.

8

MOULDED VENEER HULLS

SYNTHETIC resin glues have made possible the moulding
of shapes from layers of veneer, carrying laminating a
stage further. If strips of veneer are used it becomes
possible to make shapes with a limited amount of double
curvature. What is being done is the manufacture of a
piece of plywood in the shape desired instead of as a flat
sheet. In this way it is possible to build up the hull of a
boat—in effect, making a piece of plywood in the shape
of a boat.

No one name has become generally accepted for the
process. Common names are 'cold moulded' and 'hot
moulded' hulls. In the first, the glue sets at ordinary temperatures. In the second, heat and pressure are applied.
The latter ensures the strongest bond and quickens production, but the equipment needed is out of reach of an
amateur or small professional boat builder. As glass-
reinforced plastic hulls may also be described as cold
moulded, we favour using 'moulded veneer' as a
description of the process.

The boat has to be built over a mould, which can be
used for any number of boats. As the mould has to be
accurately made and is likely to take longer to make and
cost more than a boat off it, the method is really only
suitable for quantity production. However, the quantity

need not be great to justify making a mould. If a club wants six identical boats the labour and cost of making a mould, spread over six boats, will probably be justified, and the resulting craft will be better and more quickly built than if a hard-chine plywood design was chosen.

Although reverse curves are possible after a little experience has been gained, most moulded veneer hulls have no hollows in their lines. As the moulded hull has to be lifted off the mould there should be nothing in the design to prevent this; tumblehome, such as at the gunwale. If the boat is to have a transom, this need not be fitted until after the hull has been lifted from the mould, as this allows a certain amount of spring to aid removal.

The mould is made in the shape of the inside of the hull. For parts which come inside the hull and form part of its structure there must be grooves in the mould. Usually these are only the hog and stem. Gunwales, risers and other parts are fitted after the hull has been lifted off the mould. The mould does not need to have a completely solid surface, as it does for glass-reinforced plastic moulding, but any gaps should not be more than about $\frac{1}{2}$ in. Moulds are usually made with formers and lengthwise laths.

Unless there is no doubt about being able to leave the mould fixed down until all boats are built, it is advisable to make it rigid enough in itself to keep its shape if moved about. For a small dinghy this can be achieved by building the mould on two parallel pieces of 4 in. × 2 in. deal. The canoe mould in some of the photographs is on only one piece, but this craft is only 23 in. beam. The whole mould should have individual parts stiff enough to withstand local pressure without distorting. Formers may be deal, say from 6 in. × $\frac{3}{4}$ in. floorboarding for a dinghy. Lengthwise parts should be stiff enough, but their size depends on how close the formers are. With formers 18 in. apart they might be ¾ in. square. If a mould is built and then the surface is found to be not stiff enough, thin strips of ash, like timbers, may be bent around inside.

To make this type of mould, erect the formers on the base pieces and fix the shape which will come inside the stem. Add the lengthwise pieces which come each side of the hog (fig. 29A). If the hog is not the same thickness as the strips the formers should be notched or provided with packings to bring it level. Fix the 'gunwales'. Further strips should be arranged, as many as can be got on to the end pieces with little or no tapering (fig. 29B). These should be evenly spaced around the centre former, with gaps which will take two or more strips (fig. 29C). The structure at this stage looks very much like the framework of a fabric-covered canoe.

Fill the gaps with more strips taken as far towards the ends as possible, then tapered and cut off. It may be necessary to put in more thin strips for short distances around the middle of the boat so as to fill any gaps which are still too wide. It is possible to build a hull on a mould with quite wide gaps, but keeping the gaps narrow makes the work easier and more accurate and limits the amount of glue which finds its way between the veneer strips and has to be cleaned off later (plate 14).

The outside of the mould should be trued up. Ridges between strips must be removed and the final curve should be fair in all directions. However, the surface need not be very smooth. A Surform tool used diagonally will quickly level off ridges, but it leaves fairly coarse scratches, and these do not matter.

At the stern of a boat with a transom there need be no special preparation, but at the stem, or both ends of a canoe, there has to be a shaped part to take the veneers. This can be three strips laminated and spliced to the hog

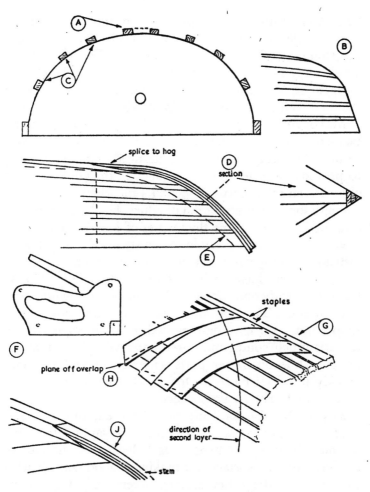

FIG. 29. Constructional details of a moulded-veneer hull

(fig. 29D). They can be held to the mould by screws while the glue sets. The mould could be notched to take a solid stem (fig. 29E). The important thing is that the mould should be faired off to meet this, then the stem and the end of the hog should be faired off to match after its glue has set. The hog may be put into position and temporarily screwed to formers or blocks inside the mould and the stem laminating done in position. The end of the mould may be greased to prevent any glue sticking these parts to it. Elsewhere on the mould polythene sheet is more convenient for preventing sticking.

Mahogany veneers are usual, although other woods can be used. The minimum thickness for easy working is about $1\frac{1}{2}$ mm. Anything thinner than this needs careful handling to prevent damage and air pockets. A thickness of three of these veneers is between $\frac{3}{16}$ and $\frac{1}{4}$ in. which has enough strength for canoes and small dinghies. For larger dinghies and small cruisers three thicknesses of $\frac{1}{8}$ in. are adequate. Above this size it is possible to use strips of thin plywood instead of a larger number of thinner veneers.

The veneers have to be cut into strips. They can be bought already cut or may be cut with a knife and straight-edge. The best width to choose depends on the shape, but 3 in. may be regarded as an average. Where there is much compound curve narrower pieces may be better, while on flatter parts wider strips will be more quickly fitted. If pieces of too great a width are chosen there is more risk of air pockets.

Any synthetic resin glue may be used, but a single-application glue is less trouble than a two-application one, as the labour of applying it is halved and the risk of hardener on one surface not making a good contact with the glue on the other surface is removed. Of course, sufficient glue must always be used, but with a little experience it is possible to make a given amount of glue go further, reducing the amount of surplus glue to be removed and giving a slightly lighter and cheaper hull.

Veneers have to be held to the mould and to each other while the glue sets. Light tacks have been used, but the most convenient things are wire staples, as used in offices for joining papers. They can be driven with an office stapler, with its base turned back, but the ideal tool is a trigger tacker (fig. 29F and plate 15), as used for fixing labels on packing cases. A spring drives the staple as the lever is pressed.

Before fixing the first skin, cover the mould, but not the hog, with pieces of polythene sheeting. Use a few staples if necessary.

Cut the end of a strip of veneer to about 45 deg. (with scissors if thin). Have a centre line on the hog. Near the middle of the boat, put glue on the hog and staple the cut end of the veneer against the line (fig. 29G). Pull the strip around the mould and staple it to the lower edge. Cut off the surplus just below the edge of the mould. Try another strip beside it. On the moderate curves at the middle of most boats it will fit without attention to its edge. Fix this in the same way. It may be possible to fix another parallel piece, then the next one will tend to ride over the previous one as it is tried. Ease this edge with a plane until it fits (fig. 29H). A small block plane held in one hand is convenient for this purpose. Continue in this way from the middle towards the ends on both sides. Short pieces cut from the middle parts may be used towards the ends. At the stem, fix with staples, trimming the veneers to an approximate outline. If the end of a veneer comes at a temporary screw through the hog, notch around it so that the screw is still accessible.

Let the glue set and take out staples into the hog (a screwdriver with a thin edge is a useful tool). If there are any lumps of glue level them off. Put on a second skin, laid diagonally the other way. Start near the middle of the boat and work towards the ends. As a strip is prepared for a position, remove any staples in the first skin that would come under it. Put glue on the strip, then staple it along the hog and press it down, working from there towards the gunwale and putting staples where necessary. Rub down well to squeeze out air. Leave the boat for the glue to set.

Remove all the staples through the second skin. Withdraw any screws through stem and hog. Clean off any lumps of glue. Fix a third layer diagonally the same way as the first. Leave this for the glue to set.

Remove all staples. Clean off surplus glue. Trim the edges of veneers around the stem. In some woods the tiny staple holes will close up without attention, but to ensure them doing so, wipe over the outside once or twice with hot water. Use the edge of the mould as a guide for drawing a pencil line around the gunwale. Remove the boat from the mould. Clean off surplus glue inside.

It is unlikely that the hull will distort after removal, but at this stage be careful how it is handled. Support it evenly and symmetrically. Fix the gunwales fairly soon after removal from the mould and trim the edges to them. If necessary, put a temporary strip across the gunwales while work is done on the hull. An external strip may form a keel and be continued by laminations around the stem (fig. 29J).

This method of building is quite easy and the veneering can be done successfully by people otherwise unskilled at woodwork. The strength of the finished hull is in the skin and no internal structure is needed to keep its shape. Veneers and glue cost less than the materials needed for most other methods of building. A capacity for taking care is more important than skill at woodwork.

Sometimes a veneer shows a blister after the glue has set, indicating that there is an air pocket inside. If this happens the blister can be slit along the grain with a sharp knife, some glue inserted, then staples used. When cleaned off, the treatment should be almost invisible.

Removing staples can be rather tedious. Driving them

over a length of string may be tried. Tape is better. This
can be pulled to release at least one leg of the staple. If
there is difficulty in making a veneer lie down, a staple
may be driven through a scrap piece of veneer or card.
Other methods of veneering are possible. They may be
taken around the boat from gunwale to gunwale in one
piece and the hog omitted, but this involves careful
trimming of long pieces. The two inner layers may be
laid diagonally and the outer layer put on fore and aft.
Except for appearance, there is no advantage in this and
it involves more trimming. Length is made up by butting
strips together. Inner and outer skins may be laid diagonally, but the middle layer put on with strips across the
boat from gunwale to gunwale at right angles to the
centre line. Inner and outer layers should be without
joins in their length between hog and gunwale, but for
economy short lengths may be used up in the middle
layer without affecting the strength of the hull.

Veneer is cut on a machine like a lathe, which takes a
shaving off a revolving log. This flattened shaving is the
veneer, but the method of cutting has the effect of opening
the grain. This means that it tends to attract dirt. Consequently it is inadvisable to leave the surface unvarnished
too long. As soon as keel, stem, transom, rubbing strips or
other parts have been fixed outside, all of the outer surface
should be given at least one coat of varnish before working
on the inside. Of course, if the final finish is paint,
protection from dirt is not so important.

9

GLASS-FIBRE CONSTRUCTION

This is, undoubtedly, the method of the future for commercial building of small-craft hulls. Instead of building up the hull from a great many pieces, the whole thing is moulded in one piece without joints which might eventually be the cause of leaks. Beside complete waterproofness, the hull is immune to most things which attack wood and metal and it has a remarkable strength. If maintenance is neglected the life and strength are unaffected, although appearance may suffer.

There is some confusion about the name. 'Fibre glass' is the word best known and most commonly used by the public, but this is really the trade name of a make of glass-reinforcing material. In the industries using the process it is more correctly called 'Glass-reinforced plastic', often abbreviated to the initials 'G.R.P.' This is a better description of the process. If the trade name is to be avoided, 'glass fibre' is a suitable name and this is commonly used. It is the one adopted in this book.

To make anything from glass fibre it is first necessary to have a mould. Sometimes this can be an existing article, but more often it has to be made. The mould is coated with a parting agent to prevent the resins sticking to it. This is coated with a synthetic resin into which glass mat is bedded, then the resin is allowed to set (fig. 30A).

PLATE 14

Part of the mould for a
moulded veneer canoe,
with some of the first
strips of veneer attached.
Polythene sheeting is
used between the mould
and the veneers

PLATE 15

Using a trigger tacker to
fix strips of veneer

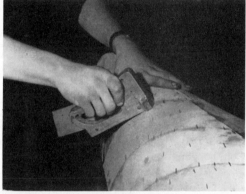

PLATE 16

Inside the moulded
veneer hull of a Fairey
Marine 'Firefly', showing
the freedom from hull
structure

PLATE 17

Above: A 22 ft. glass fibre hull being fitted out in wood as a canal cruiser. The chine has a moulded thickening piece and the dark lines are substantial wood rubbing strips. *Below:* This Mercury dinghy has a bulkhead forward of the mast and buoyancy compartments under side benches and stern sheets. Construction is unusual, with plywood sides and bottom and moulded veneer around the turn of the bilges

PLATE 18

The glass-fibre moulding is then lifted off. Its inside will be as smooth as the surface of the mould, but the outside will be rough. For a boat this would be unsatisfactory. To make a moulding with a smooth exterior, the next step is to support the first moulding the right way up and repeat the process inside—coating with parting agent and laying up resin and glass mat (fig. 30B). When this has set and been lifted out, it will have a smooth exterior and a rough interior. This is the moulding which will be used as a hull. Of course, any number of hulls may be made from the

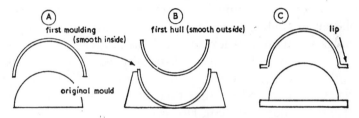

FIG. 30. Steps in glass-fibre moulding

first moulding, and this is the technique used for quantity production in industry.

The main snag for an amateur wanting only one hull is the cost and labour of making the first mould and the glass-fibre moulding from it before he starts on the boat hull itself. Materials are comparatively expensive, and for most workers the process does not become economically possible until a dozen or more hulls are required and the first costs can be spread over them.

One attraction of the process is that almost any shape is possible. This means that flared hulls, twin hulls, complete cabin and deck mouldings and mouldings which incorporate several parts are possible. Several of these would be very difficult or impossible to produce by any other method. There are some flared-hull sailing dinghies, and fast motor boats with unusual hulls produced commercially, which could not be made from any other material. Of course, the original mould may then be a complicated and difficult thing to make, but a large production from it justifies this.

Moulds

Making a glass-fibre article does not involve pressures which require great strength in the mould, so the mould can be made of almost any material. For small items plaster, modelling clay, flexible plastics and similar shaped things are used, but for an article as large as a boat, the main structure of the mould is usually wood. This can be made in the same way as that for a moulded veneer hull (fig. 29A, B, C) except that there is no need to allow for letting in a hog and stem. However, there must be no gaps in the mould. This means fitting the wooden strips more accurately, although final filling may be done with plaster.

Glass fibre will reproduce every mark on the surface of the mould so great care is needed sanding the mould smooth. This should be followed by varnishing or painting several coats, with each coat sanded well. Follow this with wax polish. Time spent on bringing this male mould to a high finish will be repaid in the saving in time finishing the female mould.

The male mould may be carried higher than the gunwale line, to allow for trimming the rough edge later. To give stiffness and to prevent the final hull losing shape before it receives its internal structure it is worth while allowing for a lip along the gunwale line by having the male mould mounted on a flat base (fig. 30C).

Suppliers of materials have release or parting agents and it is advisable to get all materials from the same supplier so as to ensure they match and can be used together. Apply the release agent according to the maker's instructions. Thorough covering is important, as nothing can be done when a moulding will not come away from a mould, except destroy one or both.

Resins and glass

The resins commonly used are supplied as a syrup which has a limited shelf life. Kept reasonably cool and in the dark this may be almost a year, but in warm sunshine life may only be days. The resin is set by the addition of a catalyst, similar to the synthetic resin glues. However, heat is required and this is supplied by also adding an accelerator. Chemical action between this and the catalyst generates sufficient heat to set the resin. At normal temperatures the mixture has to be used fairly quickly before it quite suddenly starts to 'gel', i.e. change from a syrup which can be poured and brushed to a sort of jelly. This means that only sufficient to use in the period specified by the suppliers should be mixed at one time. Nothing can be done to resoften any mixture which gels in the pot.

The ordinary resin sets translucent. To this are added fillers and pigments. They make the casting opaque and give it a colour, but there are other reasons for adding them. In boats the filler is usually a powder, which cheapens production and gives an increase in compressive strength. One problem in laying up with resin is stopping it running off near vertical surfaces. This is done by adding a thixotropic filler. As this is difficult to mix as a powder, it is also supplied ready-mixed in resin for adding to the main mix.

To give colour pigments for most colours are available, preferably already ground into some resin which is added to the main mix. The quantity required is quite small. It is also possible to use dry powders.

Suppliers of materials provide instructions and their advice about proportions should be followed closely. Casual mixing of approximate quantities may result in something which always remains sticky or sets so quickly that the mixture cannot be used.

Glass fibre is supplied in a form like a natural cloth. If it is examined closely, the strands will be seen to be made up of a great number of exceedingly thin filaments. The cloth may be in wide pieces or narrow tapes. The material may be woven in several patterns in the same way as ordinary cloth. A fairly loose plain weave is usually all that is needed in boat building. Besides woven cloths there are mats made up of short strands forming no particular pattern and loosely bonded to each other with an adhesive, which dissolves into the resin as this 'chopped strand mat' is laid up.

Woven cloths are fairly costly, so mats are mainly used for cheapness. Their strength is not as good, but for many purposes it is adequate. Tapes are dearer than cloths, but for narrow shaped work and bonding in other materials they are essential. Stiffness of a particular shape is largely dependent on total thickness. Several layers of glass fibre may be used, and may be needed to provide strength, but glass is much more expensive than resin, so where thickness is needed for stiffness, and strength is already adequate, more resin and filler are used. The designer of a boat intended to be built in glass fibre may specify the amount of glass fibre and resin to be used, or the suppliers of materials can recommend suitable combinations.

Moulding

The process of moulding is usually described as 'laying up'. Suppliers may provide instructions, but briefly the steps are as follows, whether making a female mould or the actual hull in it. A 'gel coat' of resin mixture is applied first by brush. This provides the smooth surface and keeps the glass fibre under a thin layer of resin. As this gels cloth is pressed into it and more resin added. A stippling action with a brush drives out air bubbles. Special rollers may be bought for pressing in the cloth. This can be followed by more cloth or mat and resin.

Although the resin quickly gels and may be hard to the touch after a day, it does not gain its full strength and rigidity for many days. It is therefore advisable to leave the moulding in place on the mould for a week to 'cure' before attempting to remove it. A female mould has to be made sufficiently rigid to prevent it distorting. This can be done with a wooden structure forming legs or a sort of scaffolding. Wood can be bonded to the mould with resin and cloth. Any bad spots in a female mould can be rubbed down with wet-and-dry paper followed by metal polish.

Glass fibre and wood

Glass fibre and resin will bond to wood. Although the makers do not offer a 100% certainty in all circumstances, in practice the bond is adequate. A wooden hull may be completely sheathed in glass fibre. This is best done when the boat is new. If an existing boat is sheathed it must first be cleaned off down to the bare wood. Complete sheathing up to the gunwales is advised, or at least to well above the water-line. Several firms supply complete kits for this job and their instructions should be followed, but all that has to be done is coat the wood with a resin mix and cover this with glass-fibre cloth and more resin. Of course, the outside does not have the perfection which is possible when the material is cast in a mould, but by careful brushing followed by sanding and polishing it is possible to achieve a surface acceptable for most purposes.

Glass-fibre tape and resin may be used to strengthen and waterproof joints in plywood construction. The chine is covered with tape and resin outside (fig. 31A) before the new boat is painted or varnished. This may be done as an

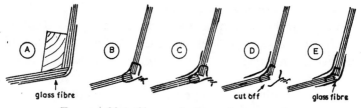

FIG. 31. Glass-fibre and plywood construction

additional process to any plywood boat, and is worth while for a boat likely to get rough treatment or frequent jarring during extensive trailing.

A further step is to use the glass-fibre tape and resin to make the joint between plywood parts. This produces a very light structure. There is little rigidity in the joint itself, but this is a possible construction when the boat is designed so that the hull is well braced by built-in buoyancy or other internal structure.

Boats have been built in this way by supporting the plywood panels in contact while the resin sets, but this is rather tedious and some means of holding the plywood edges together temporarily by fastenings is better. The method is particularly suitable for very light construction, using thin plywood. Examples are the Kayel series of kayaks and the 'Mirror' sailing dinghy.

Edges are tied together. Plastic fishing line has possibilities, or copper wire may be used. The edges are pulled together with wire through holes spaced close enough to hold the parts in shape—probably 4 in. to 8 in. on most edges (fig. 31B). Resin and tape are applied inside and left to set (fig. 31C). Excess wire is cut off outside and the ends filed level (fig. 31D). More tape and resin is applied outside (fig. 31E). Edges need not mate perfectly, in fact a small gap through which the resin may flow and unite with that on the other side is a good thing. It is possible to make a stem in the same way, although some additional stiffness may be desirable. Wood bonded in with resin and tape will do. It is also possible to cast a stem in a mould, with resin and glass 'rovings' (oddments of glass strands).

Methods of attaching wood to glass fibre when fitting out the hull are described in Chapter 10.

10

INTERNAL WORK

T HE building of the hull of a boat often goes ahead faster
than had been anticipated and there is soon something to
show for the work put into it. This engenders a feeling
that the job is almost completed, when, in fact, it may not
be half done. Dealing with the internal work of even a
fairly simple open boat may take longer than expected,
while the fitting out of the inside of a cabin boat is very
time-consuming.

The fitting of thwarts and knees was dealt with in
Chapter 5 and plate 5. These are fitted in a very similar
way in any wood boat whatever its method of construction. Bottom boards are important in most boats. It is
unwise to walk or put loads directly on the skin. Bottom
boards take a local load and distribute it. In a small open
boat it is an advantage to let the bottom boards curve
(Chapter 5), as this keeps the load low and makes the
small boat as roomy as possible. In runabouts and larger
craft, flat bottom boards are more usual. They can be
plywood, with stiffeners below (fig. 32A), and should be
removable in sections. It is bad policy to have any part
of the hull inaccessible inside in emergency. Lifting boards
also allow bailing and removal of rubbish. So that bilge
water can run to the lowest point, waterways (limber
holes) should be provided beside the hog, in every frame
or other cross member (fig. 32B).

Many modern boats are built extremely lightly compared with craft built up to about the early 1950s. In many cases the internal arrangement of thwarts, lockers, buoyancy compartments, bulkheads or other things which might be thought of as additions are really essential parts of the whole structure (plates 16, 18). If a published design is to be modified, this fact should be taken into account and other strength members used if a part is left out.

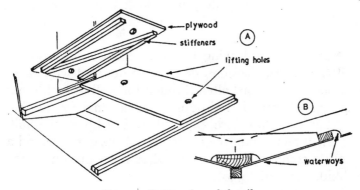

FIG. 32. Bottom-board details

Decking braces the whole hull and prevents distortion. Fore and side decks bonded to the gunwales are strength members, even if they also serve other purposes. If the gunwale is stout enough, a beam to support the foredeck may be notched into it (fig. 33A), but with modern glues to help, it is probably stronger to fix it to a block and avoid weakening the gunwale by cutting (fig. 33B). This sort of construction, which may seem crude to the traditional craftsman, is quite satisfactory with modern materials. In a very small dinghy a piece of plywood bent over the beam and the gunwales will be stiff enough to support itself (fig. 33C). If there is to be a bollard or other fitting to take a load, a king plank should go under the deck (fig. 33D and plate 19). On a large deck there may be other fore and aft supports.

Side decking rests on the gunwales and inner strips called 'carlins'. Brackets from the frames may support the side decks. Make all of the deck framing before starting to cover any part, then fair it off, including the gunwales. In an open boat with side decking the deck ply may cover the side ply and, in turn, be covered by a rubbing strip (fig. 33E). Everything should be bedded in glue. Brass nails or barbed ring alloy nails look better than screw heads in decking, particularly if spaced evenly and parallel to the edges.

When wooden decking has to be fixed to a glass-fibre hull (plate 17), the gunwale may be doubled with strips of wood screwed or bolted through the hull to each other (fig. 33F). Synthetic resin glue does not make a satisfactory bond to glass fibre, but if there is a lip on the hull, glue may be used on the inner part of the gunwale and a jointing compound put on the glass fibre and under the rubbing strip (fig. 33G).

There may be a coaming around the edge of the deck (plate 20). Exposed edges should be rounded (fig. 33H). Cabin sides may be fixed in the same way, but the carlin will have to be bevelled (fig. 33J and plate 21).

Varnished or painted plywood does not give a very safe foothold. On larger craft decks may be covered with canvas. Some paint makers supply a special compound or paint for putting on the wood, then the canvas is stretched and fixed while this is wet. It is important that the canvas covers without a break. If it is necessary to join to make up an area, an adhesive should be used. Fittings should be removed and fixed over the canvas. Cutting around anything makes an opening into which water may creep and start rot. If the canvas is to come against a vertical surface, it should be turned up and covered with a moulding

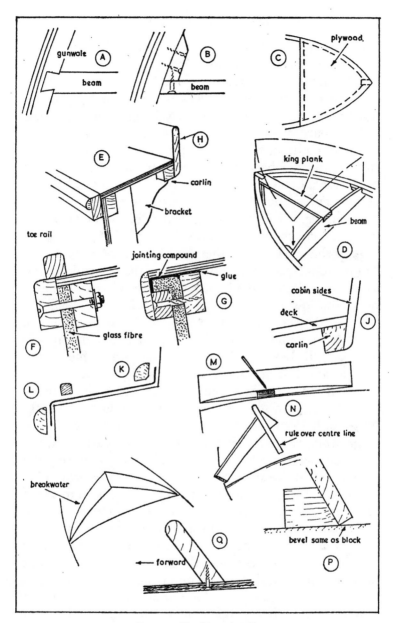

FIG. 33. Decking details

(fig. 33K). At outer edges it should be turned down and may be covered by a rubbing strip (fig. 33L). There are plastic paints which serve a similar purpose, but are easier to apply.

A breakwater on the foredeck has some tricky angles if it is to look right. A template may be made from a piece of hardboard, rather larger than the finished job is to be. Put it in position, possibly with a block to hold it at the correct angle. Check the widest gap under its straight edge. Use a block of this width with a pencil to mark the bottom curve (fig. 33M). Cut this and try the piece in position. Sight from above the centre line of the deck and mark and cut the central mitre (fig. 33N). Trim the upper edge to shape and mark the pair of pieces of wood which will make the actual breakwater. Cut the top and bottom to shape, but leave some waste where the pieces will meet. Bevel the lower edges, using the block which held the hardboard as a guide (fig. 33P). At the centre, cut the mitre by eye and try the parts together in position, adjusting until they fit. Mark where the parts come on the deck and drill from below for screws (fig. 33Q).

In a small cabin boat the decking is fixed, followed by the cabin sides, which usually continue to form the cockpit sides. Bottom boards, or cabin sole, should be built in fairly soon, so that it is possible to work inside without doing damage with local weights. If there are frames, the design will indicate how the boards are to be arranged; the frames giving a convenient datum to work from to get them level. If there are no frames, measurements must be taken down from the gunwales and forward from the corners of the transom. It may be necessary to fit one or more main bulkheads before the bottom boards. If so, put in temporary boards to walk on at this stage.

If much work has to be done from inside the boat, the hull must be supported adequately. The main load should be taken under the keel at several points. Supports should come under the skin at frames or chines—not below un-stiffened parts of plywood panels. If there is a trailer intended for the particular boat, it may be possible to work on that. Struts may also come from the gunwales to workshop floor or wall.

See that you are not likely to tilt the boat when you transfer your weight to one part. Be careful that undue force to make a part fit is not, in fact, forcing the hull to the shape of the part. Until the hull is well braced by internal structure this is a possibility, even with a large hull. Sight along the hull when it is set up and check from time to time. Any twist or distortion can usually be seen. If the design indicates the position of the water-line it is useful to use this as a guide to setting the boat up horizontally with the aid of a spirit level. It should, of course, be horizontal when checked transversely. While a horizontal set-up in a fore-and-aft direction is not essential, it is a help in checking the level of bunk tops and bottom boards as a spirit level can be used.

In a cabin boat there is at least one bulkhead, which has to be set up true. The parts each side of the door or hatch can usually be cut from sheet plywood without joints, but the shape is fairly complicated. If the bulkhead is on a frame, this may be used as a guide, but fitting is best done from a strip across the gunwales or tops of the cabin sides, with another strip arranged with one edge vertical over the centre line or door edge. The shape around the edge can be found by spiling (fig. 13E, F, G, and Chapter 4). From this it will probably be best to mark out a hardboard template. Check the piece in the other side and mark out both pieces of plywood.

The cabin structures of small boats can usually be made up by framing up plywood with strips nailed and glued on. Strips about $\frac{7}{8}$ in. square around a piece of 8 mm plywood, all bonded together with synthetic resin glue, make a surprisingly strong unit (fig. 34A). This may seem crude by traditional cabinet-making standards, but the strength is in the plywood and the framing is mainly used for stiffness rather than structural strength (plate 22). At corners the framing may be cut back to make a notch for another part (fig. 34B). Places where a dovetail or a

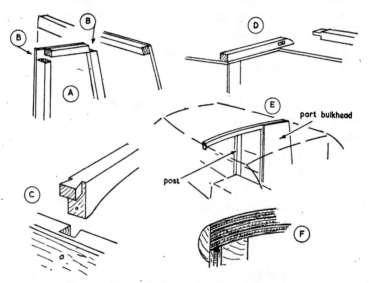

FIG. 34. Framed-plywood cabin construction

mortise and tenon joint may be favoured are where there could be a tendency to spread. The ends of cabin roof beams might be dovetailed (fig. 34c). The structure around a hatch or doorway could be tenoned (fig. 34D) to make a workmanlike job.

Headroom in a small cabin boat is not usually sufficient to allow standing, unless it is a sea-going boat over about 30 ft. or an inland boat over about 24 ft. Attempting to get standing headroom in a small boat is the cause of more ugly craft than anything else. To give as much clearance as possible cabin roof beams are made as shallow as possible and well rounded. Quite often they can be reinforced by such things as part bulkheads or a post between galley and bunk (fig. 34E). With these things to reduce the unsupported spans, lighter structures can be used. Another way of strengthening the cabin top while keeping the internal structure to a minimum is to laminate it. Two, or even three, thin sheets of plywood are glued together in position (fig. 34F). The greater the

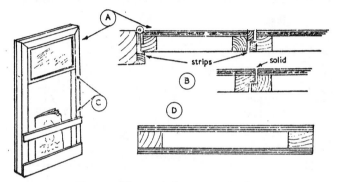

FIG. 35. Plywood-door construction

curve, the stronger will be this type of cabin top. For some purposes there could be sufficient strength in the laminated plywood, so that no final framing is needed, although a temporary frame or mould will be needed for shaping. The biggest problem in building up this type of cabin top by hand work is the avoidance of air gaps, which would make weak places. Weights and cramps should be used, but there may also have to be some nails.

Small doors may be stiffened plywood (fig. 35A). Although rebates can be planed for framing or meeting edges (fig. 35B), glued-on strips are just as satisfactory and easy to apply. The inside of the door may take a mirror or a book rack (fig. 35C), thus making use of all available space, but if this type of assembly is too light there is a risk of the door warping. This can be reduced by panelling the door both sides (fig. 35D).

Windows in a cabin boat may be made in several ways. There is a tendency for windows to become larger, but normally they do not provide strength and care is needed to see that what is left after cutting out window openings is adequate (plate 21). Complete window units may be bought, but they may be expensive and designed originally for caravans, in a metal which will not stand up to

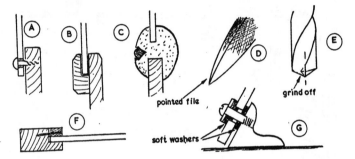

FIG. 36. Fitting Perspex

salt-water conditions. It is more usual, and quite satisfactory, to make the windows from Perspex. Any outline is easily cut and any slight twist or curve in the cabin side can be followed.

Perspex may be screwed to the wood over a jointing compound (fig. 36A) or enclosed in a wooden frame (fig. 36B), but the neatest way of obtaining a workmanlike and watertight finish is to use a rubber moulding. Most popular is a type which has a strip inserted to make the rubber grip both Perspex and plywood (fig. 36C). Most of these mouldings are made by Clayton-Wright, Wellesbourne, Warwick, and obtainable through chandlers. A special tool is used to insert the strip, but this is cheap and may sometimes be hired from the moulding supplier.

Transparent Perspex is supplied with the surfaces protected with paper lightly stuck on. This should be left on until immediately before fitting, to prevent scratches and to provide a surface for marking out. Cut with a hand saw. A coping saw will cut curves. Support near the cut to avoid cracks. Trim edges with a fairly coarse file. If the edge is to be exposed, follow with glasspaper. If fitting in a moulding, a slight bevel all round is a help in inserting.

Perspex tends to be brittle in very cold conditions, so it is always more easily worked and less likely to crack in a warm room, or outside on a sunny day. Moderate curves in windows may be sprung cold, but if an intricate shape is wanted, some transparent Perspex will soften in boiling water, but most of it and the coloured material needs the heat of a domestic oven. It can be made as limp as cloth, but its surface is then easily marked, and chamois leather is about the only material safe to use for handling or covering moulds. Seams in gloves or the weave in cloth will mark the soft plastic.

Perspex may be drilled with small metalworking twist drills, used in a hand-operated wheel-brace, with light pressure. An electric drill may generate too much heat by friction and make a ragged hole. A centre for starting the drill is best made with a few turns of a triangular-pointed tool (fig. 36D). Support the Perspex directly under the drill. For holes above about $\frac{3}{16}$ in. the leading edges of the drill should be ground vertical (fig. 36E). If this is not done there is a risk of the drill pulling in and seizing so as to crack the plastic.

If the manufactured surface is undamaged and the edges are covered there is no need to polish the Perspex, but if the surface becomes scratched or a cut edge has to be polished, this can be treated with metal polish, or one of the special polishes obtainable from the Perspex supplier. After fine glasspaper, follow with a brass polish and then one intended for silver. The shine is obtained by breaking down the surface with successively finer abrasives, so do not start with anything coarser than is necessary. If anything has to be built up from Perspex parts the only satisfactory adhesive is Perspex cement, which is Perspex in a liquid form and the joint made is really a weld. Perspex knobs or handles can be fixed in this way.

Holes for screws or other fixings should be oversize. A crack may develop if the neck of a screw is too close a fit. A Perspex windscreen for a cruiser may have a wooden frame, with the plastic held by wood strips (fig. 36F). For a runabout the Perspex may be self-supporting. There are special mouldings and brackets for mounting, but care is needed to avoid too rigid a fixture. For this sort of mounting, holes should be oversize and rubber, fibre or plastic washers or moulding put beneath screw heads and nuts (fig. 36G). Otherwise, vibration and changes in temperature may cause cracking.

In the upper works of a cabin boat places where water could settle and penetrate the end grain of plywood should be avoided, particularly if the finish is varnish. Where two parts meet, the upper should overlap the lower. A cabin top overlapping the sides should ensure most water falling clear of the joint (fig. 37A). Where the edge has to finish flush, the joint should be thoroughly glued.

There is no reason today for fitting planked decks on amateur-built craft, except for the sake of appearance. Teak decking with black seams certainly gives a high-class appearance. Traditional planking is narrow and deep, notched into a covering board around the gunwales, and with seams filled with marine glue or one of

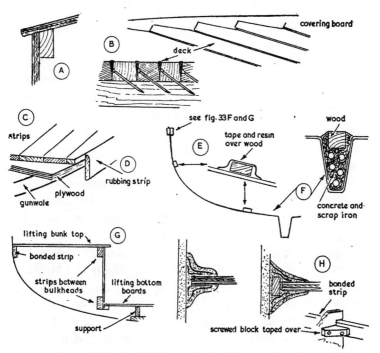

FIG. 37. Planked decks and attaching to glass fibre

the more recent mastics (fig. 37B). If done well, this is satisfactory, but the working of a boat may cause seams to open and leaks to occur. This type of decking does not provide much stiffness.

Structurally, and for thorough waterproofness, it is better to have plywood decking bonded with glue and nails or screws to all parts of the framing it touches. This may be covered with canvas or treated to make it non-slip. If a planked appearance is wanted, it is possible to get plywood on which the upper ply has dummy seams marked. This looks quite smart on the decking of a run-about. An alternative is to lay thinner planking over ply-wood (fig. 37c). Notching the ends into a covering board can be avoided if the trimmed edge is covered by a rubbing strip (fig. 37D).

When a glass-fibre hull is fitted out, holes through the skin should be avoided as far as possible, so as to retain the absolute waterproofness of this method of construction. There may have to be skin fittings for engine water intake, toilet and similar things. Properly installed these are no trouble, but holes for screws into bulkheads and other internal framing could develop leaks due to working of the boat slackening the fastenings slightly. It is better to rely on bonding wood parts to the glass fibre with resin and tape. If the design permits, there may be lengthwise wooden parts bonded to the hull, to which bulkheads, bunk framing, lockers and similar things can be screwed (fig. 37E). A hollow keel, which can be filled with iron scrap and concrete, may have a piece of wood for fastenings (fig. 37F). Direct local loads on the hull should be avoided. Instead, some major parts may be bonded to the hull, then other parts supported on them, rather than against the hull. For instance, bulkheads and the main framing for the outer edges of bunks may be bonded to the hull, then bunk framing built out and supports for the cabin bottom boards put on the bunk fronts rather than against the hull, although there may also be a central support (fig. 37G).

When using resin and tape to bond wood parts, the inside of the hull should be cleaned off with a solvent and the surface sanded immediately before making the joint. The unprepared surface tends to be greasy and attracts dirt, so that a good bond is unlikely. Edgewise joints can be made with resin and tape fillets. Strips are better bonded by wrapping the glass over them. Several methods are shown (fig. 37H).

II

SAILING GEAR

COMPARED with a pulling or outboard boat of the same size, the building of a sailing boat involves about twice as much work. Mast and spars have to be made, although manufactured metal masts are favoured for some classes of sailing boat. Sails are usually professionally made. Structure to support the mast has to be built in. There must be a rudder—controlled by a tiller in all but the largest boats. Additional keel surface has to be provided, and it is this which involves the greatest amount of additional work.

If the boat has a central deep-ballasted fixed keel, the work involved tends to be heavy and call for more equipment than most amateurs and many boat builders possess. For lengthy voyages in open water this type of yacht hull is favoured, but for other conditions it is unlikely to be chosen. In harbours which dry out it has to be provided with legs. The alternative fixed-keel arrangement is to have twin bilge keels. These, sometimes with a skeg aft, allow the boat to sit upright when it takes the bottom. Building a boat with bilge keels only involves providing sufficient internal structure to take the load over the keels, which are usually made up by welding sheet steel and bolted on over a jointing compound (fig. 38A and plates 23, 24).

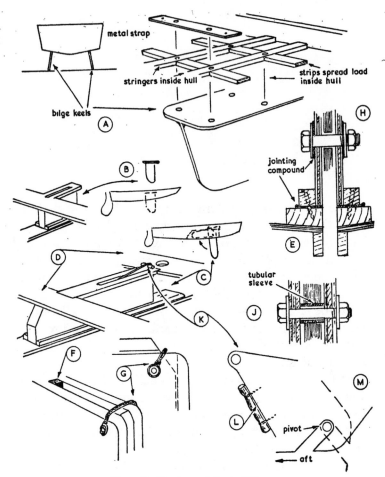

FIG. 38. Keels and their fitting

If the keel is to retract into the hull, it may be a dagger board, in the smallest dinghies and some catamarans, which lifts up and down in a waterproof case (fig. 38B and plate 13); or a centreboard, which is pivoted so as to swing up into its case (fig. 38c and plates 9, 25). There is considerable sideways pressure when the boat is sailing on some points and this must be allowed for when fitting the case. Whenever possible, the case should be braced by cross-members, usually two thwarts in an open boat (fig. 38D). If this is done there can be little movement, but to allow for possible working it is usual to bed down the case on a jointing compound, instead of glue which sets rigid.

To fit a case, make it up as a unit, but paint the inside during assembly as this is difficult to get at later. Shape the bottom to fit against the hog as accurately as possible. Cut the slot in the bottom undersize. Drill holes for fixing screws and coat the bottom of the box with jointing compound. Screw down, working progressively all round so that the jointing compound squeezes out fairly evenly (fig. 38E). Finally trim the slot to match the inside of the case.

A problem with a dagger board is making it stay down under normal circumstances, but able to ride up if it hits the bottom. Plastic or rubber foam in the case ends may provide sufficient friction (fig. 38F). A piece of shock cord looped over a sloping end of the top will also do the job (fig. 38G).

The pivot for a centreboard usually comes below the waterline and may cause leaks. Jointing compound may be put around the bolt and under washers (fig. 38H). Rubber washers may be used. Excessive tightening may pinch the centreboard. It is better to put a sleeve on the bolt, although assembly may be rather difficult (fig. 38J). Centreboards are usually made of plywood. An extension forming a handle is all that is needed to raise or lower (fig. 38K). Friction to hold the board at any angle can be provided by squeezing a short length of rubber or plastic hose (fig. 38L). If the board is metal, tackle may be needed to raise it or hold it in any position. Gravity will lower it. One advantage of fitting a metal centreplate is that it can be slotted over its pivot and the risk of leaks there is reduced (fig. 38M).

The simplest rudder is a board hinged to the stern, with a tiller mortised over the top (fig. 39A). It is more

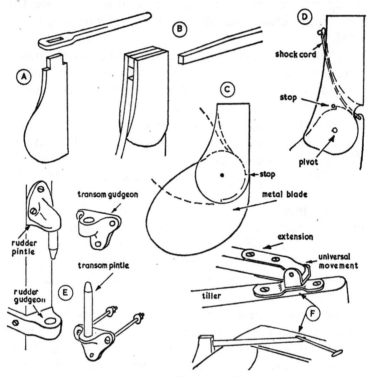

FIG. 39. Rudders and tillers

usual to thicken the stock with cheeks, which can extend to provide a mortise into which the tiller is pushed (fig. 39B). If the blade is to lift, it may be metal so that its own weight keeps it down (fig. 39C), but more often it is plywood kept down by a piece of shock cord in tension (fig. 39D).

There are several types of rudder hangings, but most

common are gudgeons (the parts with holes) and pintles (which fit in the holes). While wood screws may be satisfactory in the rudder, it is better to have bolts through the transom for the fittings there, as considerable strain is sometimes put on these hangings (fig. 39E). For the well-known dinghy racing classes there are special sets of rudder hangings available.

To reduce the danger of the main sheet fouling the top of the rudder, it is kept low by using a metal plate, preferably stainless steel, looped over to form a housing for the tiller. There is often considerable twisting action on this point, so the plate should be very secure, with rivets or bolts.

It is worth while spending some time making the tiller comfortably rounded. In larger craft this is one place where carving or decorative ropework is not out of place. Ash or hickory stand up best to the bending strains in a straight tiller. A cranked tiller may be laminated around a former, using wood of contrasting colour (fig. 11C). In a small racing boat, where the helmsman may sit out, the tiller stick or extension should be fitted with a proper universal joint (fig. 39F).

For masts and spars the usual wood is Sitka spruce, although for cheaper utility rigs fir or pine may be used. The wood should be light and have a straight grain free from all but the smallest knots. A spar may be made from solid wood or built up by glueing several pieces (fig. 40A). In the larger sizes hollow masts may be built up. In any built-up mast there can be a groove for the main-sail luff rope (fig. 40B) and in a hollow mast halliards may pass through the mast. In a yacht electrical wiring for lighting may also pass through the mast. Building up a hollow mast needs care and skill. It is necessary to work on a long stiff straight plank or bench to ensure making the mast straight. For many racing dinghy classes the mast specified is now an aluminium alloy spar, which in general form is similar to a hollow wood mast (fig. 40c).

For working craft the mast may be a larch or fir pole with the bark scraped off, but for a dinghy or small yacht with a solid mast it is more usual to shape a piece of spruce from a square piece. This is done progressively. Plane any taper while the wood is square. On each end draw an octagon, or draw a separate square of the same size and convert that to an octagon. Draw diagonals, and measure half a diagonal, preferably with dividers, and mark this along each edge. If these points are joined the result will be a regular octagon (fig. 40D). Use these shapes as a guide to plane the corners off the spar. When the bevels are straight and can be seen to have produced eight reasonably equal surfaces, plane off the eight corners so as to leave sixteen faces.

From this stage use strips of fairly coarse glasspaper or, preferably, garnet paper to work around the wood, rubbing off the plane marks (fig. 40E). Follow this by lengthwise rubbing with finer glasspaper. The wood will soon collect dirt and lose its whiteness, so it is advisable to cut any slot for a sheave, make the tenon at the foot, drill any holes needed and generally prepare the mast immediately, then give it its first coat of varnish. Marking out around a spar, or locating the centres of a hole on opposite sides, can be done around the straight edge of a piece of paper (fig. 40F).

An oar may be made in a similar way. The shaft is tapered and pieces to make the blade glued each side (fig. 40G). The blade outline is drawn from a card template (fig. 40H), then the shaft converted to round and the blade planed to a mainly diamond section, using a centre line drawn around the edge as a guide (fig. 40J). It is usual to thin down the loom to provide a grip. This can be marked around paper (fig. 40F). A curved Surform

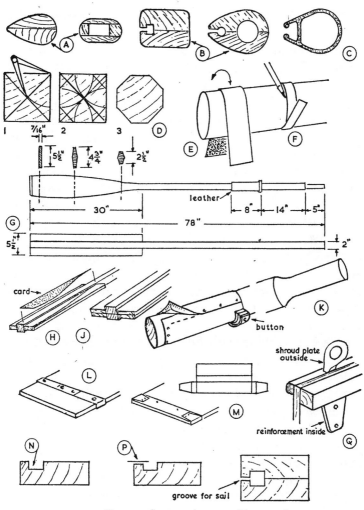

FIG. 40. Spar and oar making

tool or a rasp will hollow beside this mark, then the end is reduced (fig. 40K). The tip of the blade should be protected, either with a strip of copper nailed around (fig. 40L) or, preferably, if a soft wood has been used, with a strip wrapped over the end and riveted (fig. 40M).

Traditionally, sails were laced to spars, but it is now more usual and better aerodynamically to slide their bolt ropes along grooves. A spar is made in two pieces, which can be grooved by use of a circular saw or a plough plane (fig. 40N), then the edge thinned with a rebate plane to allow for the thickness of the sail cloth (fig. 40P). Take care to keep the spar straight when glueing and cramping and keep the cramps clear of the groove, so that a cloth can be pulled along the groove to wipe out excess glue before it has set. As with round spars, it is advisable to varnish these spruce grooved spars as soon as they have been cleaned up to prevent them absorbing dirt.

There are a great many fittings for sailing craft available, and rigging is largely a matter of following the designer's recommendations. Galvanised iron fittings tend to be crude, although cheap. Gunmetal, silicon bronze and similar alloys are preferable to common brass. Stainless steel is attractive and strong, but parts have a built-up construction as the metal is unsuitable for casting; and if holes have to be drilled in it, some grades will work-harden to such an extent that a drill which is not kept steadily cutting may blunt and have its temper drawn very quickly. Whenever possible, fittings should be bolted through rather than screwed. It may be necessary to reinforce below a deck or behind a shroud plate (fig. 40Q) so as to spread the strain over a reasonable area. Several plastics are made into fittings. In particular the brown laminated plastic, Tufnol, makes good sheaves and the sides of blocks. Hard nylon is suitable for small fairleads and similar things.

Rigging to support the mast is usually flexible steel wire, preferably stainless steel. Splicing by tucking strands is difficult in this material, and it is better to have the eye splices made by a swaging process, the best known being Talurit', or to use 'Norseman' fittings, which can be attached to the end of a wire rope with hand tools only.

For running rigging synthetic ropes have almost completely taken over from natural fibre ropes. Advantages of the man-made fibre ropes are in strength and resistance to rot. Most of them do not absorb water to any noticeable amount. Although they are naturally smooth and slippery, there are plaited and other synthetic lines for sheets and other ropes which have to be handled, which are difficult to distinguish from the hemp and manila which they replace. Although synthetic ropes cost more in the first place, their longer lives make them worth while.

Of the many synthetic ropes, Terylene has most use as a running rigging rope, being very strong and with little stretch. Nylon is used where some elasticity is an advantage. Water absorption of synthetic ropes is very slight, so rot is no problem and their characteristics are very little different when wet or dry.

The ends of plastic ropes can be sealed by heating with a flame. However it is advisable to whip them as well. Natural ropes must be whipped in any case. Light thread or line, preferably the same material as the rope, should be used. Simplest safe whipping is the West-country. A series of overhand knots is tied on opposite sides of the rope (fig. 41A) until a length of about the same as the thickness of the rope has been covered, then the last knot made into a reef knot (fig. 41B).

Ropes are often attached to shackles. Some are quick-release and several shapes are possible, but the basic pattern has a screwed pin with a hole through the end (fig. 41C). This is for securing against unscrewing, with wire, not for turning with the point of a spike. Pliers may be used, although a tool with a tapered slot, often part of a clasp knife, is better (fig. 41D). To prevent chafe the

rope is spliced around a thimble, and this eye splice is the
only one most amateurs find it necessary to master.

To make an eye splice, unlay sufficient length of strands
for tucking. Bend up a loop of the correct size with the un-
laid strands across the rope, so that they point across the

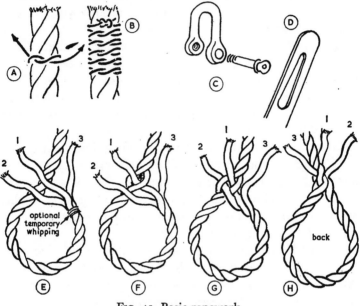

FIG. 41. Basic ropework

lay of the rope (fig. 41E). If put the wrong way they will
appear to lay in line with the laid-up strands. Tuck one
of these ends under a convenient main strand (fig. 41F).
Take the end strand which is next towards the loop, and
tuck this under the next main strand, going in where the
first came out (fig. 41G). Turn the splice over and find the
main strand still without an end under it. The remaining
end goes under this, but it must be tucked so that it points
in the same direction around the rope as the other ends
(fig. 41H). Pull up the ends evenly and, if a metal or

plastic thimble is to be included, fit it at this stage. Take each end in turn and tuck it over and under one main strand, i.e. each end goes over the next main strand around the rope and under the one after it. Do this again with each end, so that there is a total of three tucks. If the rope is very stiff, a spike may be needed to open the spaces for tucking, but soft small rope can usually be twisted open by hand.

Three full tucks should be sufficient, although for Terylene and other smooth plastic rope there may be a fourth one. For neatness, scrape away half the fibres of the remaining ends with a sharp knife, then make one more tapered tuck.

Instructions for making other knots and splices will be found in specialist knotting books (Appendix B), and some of the makers of braided ropes issue instructions for splicing them.

12

MECHANICAL INSTALLATIONS

MOST boats may have mechanical power, either permanently installed, or provided by a clamped-on outboard motor. There are very small inboard motors which can be used in quite small dinghies, but they occupy space which is already limited and there is a fair amount of installation work, so the majority of the smaller boats have outboard motors. Even where the hull seems large enough for an inboard there is an increasing tendency to use an outboard motor. Installation is much simpler and the inside of the boat is not impeded. However, as the need for power increases, running costs of a two-stroke outboard motor may become considerably more than the equivalent four-stroke inboard motor. For car-type inboard motors there are inboard/outboard drives which give the best of both worlds, but most of these are intended for higher powers. Drive is through the transom—outside is a unit very much like the lower part of an outboard motor, while inside and close to the transom is the motor. Diesel motors are considerably heavier and more costly than petrol motors of the same power. Although running costs are cheaper, the amount of running in the average pleasure boat is not usually sufficient to justify the higher initial cost, even where the extra weight is acceptable. There are jet units, which can be used instead of a propeller.

PLATE 19

Deck beam and king post ready for the plywood decking on a pram
sailing dinghy

The stern of a 17 ft. double-chine sailing cruiser. There is a moulding
between deck and coaming. A lifting panel to port allows an outboard motor
to be fitted

PLATE 20

PLATE 21

Above: The cabin structure being fitted to a small cruiser. *Below:* Internal work in the cabin of a small cruiser. Bunk fronts are attached to the main bulkhead and bottom boards will rest on the frames

PLATE 22

They do not transmit as much power as a propeller, but they have advantages in shallow or weedy water.

The outboard motor gives the least installation problem to the builder. If an inboard motor is installed conventionally there are bearers to spread the load, an exhaust system, a cooling water intake and a fuel tank, as well as the stern tube and shaft. Steering has to be by a rudder. An outboard motor acts as its own rudder. An inboard motor installed with an inboard/outboard drive needs supports, but the drive is installed via a hole in the transom, which is much simpler than using a stern tube. Fuel, cooling water and exhaust are needed. The outboard part is used for steering.

Outboard motors

For a small open boat there is usually no need for special preparation to take an outboard motor up to about 5 h.p. The majority of motors available are designed to suit a transom 15 in. deep. If there is much keel below this, it should be tapered off (fig. 42A). One of these motors may be used on a shallower transom, but on a deeper one, part of the circle covered by the propeller will be screened and power reduced. For larger boats there are long-shaft motors, usually intended for a 20 in. transom. If necessary, a transom should be notched (fig. 42B). Adjustable cramps take care of different transom angles, but modern motors are designed to suit an average angle to the horizontal of between 74 and 78 deg. (fig. 42C).

A motor when driving puts considerable strain on the transom. This should be thicker than would otherwise be needed, and the thickening piece should be carried to the sides. This will also reduce the effect of any motor vibration. Cramps on most modern motors are designed to fit

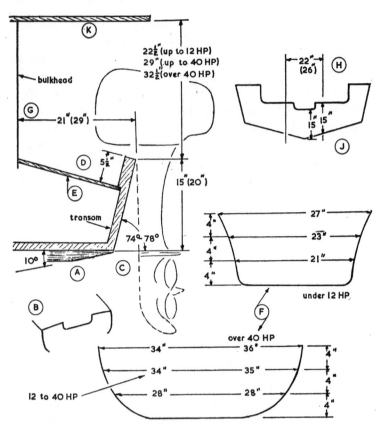

FIG. 42. Hull arrangements for outboard motors

these thicknesses of transom: up to 12 h.p. $1\frac{3}{8}$ in. to $1\frac{3}{4}$ in.; up to 40 h.p., 2 in.; over 40 h.p., $2\frac{1}{4}$ in.

There has been an attempt to standardise the fitting of motors, and most British and American motors will suit the boat sizes quoted in this chapter. The smallest motor has the fuel tank mounted on it and steering is by a tiller on the motor. For such craft as runabouts and motor cruisers it is usual to have fuel in a separate tank and there may be a battery, with a self-starter. This, with throttle and gear-shift, may be controlled remotely near a steering wheel. When this is done the boat is usually of a size where the transom has to be cut down considerably to take the water. To prevent water which may get in at this low point flooding the boat, stern decking with a motor well is needed (plate 26).

As the motor must swing through the steering arc and be able to tilt at any position, without jamming fuel pipe or control cables, the well has to be quite large. The well should be watertight, with drain holes through the transom. Any holes in the sides for controls should not be larger than necessary, kept as high as possible and sealed with rubber if possible. To allow clearance for the motor cramp, the bottom of the well should be not less than $5\frac{1}{2}$ in. from the top of the transom cut-out (fig. 42D). The bottom of the well may be at right angles to the transom, or a little steeper if locker space below is valuable (fig. 42E).

The width of the transom cut-out need not be the same throughout. There may be rounded corners. Recommended minimum widths up to 12 in. above the cramp level are shown (fig. 42F). So that the motor can tilt fully, the bulkhead should be 21 in. forward of the transom for motors up to 40 h.p. or 29 in. for motors larger than that (fig. 42G). If the bulkhead is also the back of a seat these dimensions should be increased by 3 in. so that there is no risk of a passenger's arm being caught by a tilting motor. A piece of decking may cover part of the forward edge of the well so that the tilting motor swings below it.

Sometimes a twin-motor installation is favoured. Motors up to 40 h.p. should be 22 in. apart. Larger motors should be 26 in. apart (fig. 42H). This means that cut-out widths should be increased by this amount. Other dimensions should be as for a single-motor installation. This type of installation is often used on a hull with a deep V bottom.

Then the heights should be measured at the motor centres and not over the keel. This means that if the boat is to be used occasionally with a single central motor there should be a notch at the centre to give this correct position (fig. 42J).

It is sometimes possible to arrange for the motor to be completely under a deck, but to allow clearance for tilting, this has to be quite high (fig. 42K). A lower knock-up lid is a possible alternative, but this may not be entirely satisfactory if it jams or there is anything on top when it lifts.

Accessibility of the motor is important, so any enclosing must allow access for hand starting and it should be possible to do such things as adjust the carburettor or remove sparking plugs without difficulty.

Remote steering by wheel may be central in a large craft, but in smaller cruisers it is usually to one side. For inland waters, or anywhere restricted, it is probably better on the port (left) side, where approaching craft can be observed, but in open waters, where craft may come from any direction, a view to starboard is more often needed when observing the rule of the road at sea.

Control may be cable and pulleys or an arrangement in which a flexible rod works with a push-pull action in a tube. The latter is more expensive but is easier to install. For a cable system, a flexible steel cable with plastic coating is advisable and this should work around pulleys at least 2 in. diameter, preferably mounted flexibly so that they take up the correct attitude. Very small motors may have a direct connection to the tiller or steering bracket on the motor, but for the majority of motors a 2 : 1 purchase at the motor end is advisable, with the cables anchored to the side of the boat and passing round pulleys at the motor (fig. 43A). With the usual method of attaching to the motor, the cable is at a slightly different tension at different points of the motor swing. This is taken up by a strong spring at one or both ends (fig. 43B).

In a runabout the cables may be taken along both sides of the boat (fig. 43C). In a cruiser they may pass along one side (fig. 43D). All anchorages get considerable strain when the wheel is turned suddenly. Bolts should be taken through where possible—wood screws may pull

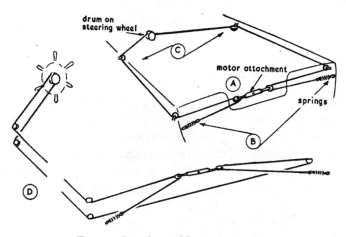

FIG. 43. Steering-cable arrangements

out. Similarly, the wheel should be securely mounted (plate 27), possibly on a thickened bulkhead, otherwise it may come away in an emergency. It should be possible to cast off the remote steering easily, usually by a quick-release connection to the motor, so that tiller steering can be used if preferred or if there is a breakdown in the remote system.

Installation instructions for remote controls for throttle and gear-shift are provided by the makers. Moderate curves are necessary if they are to work easily. This means loops at the motor end. If the well is the minimum size, care is needed to see that they do not become jammed or bent too sharply at any point that the motor can be. Most large motors have a point for attaching a safety chain. If a chain with a spring clip can be taken straight down to an eyebolt through the bottom of the well, it should be possible to arrange it so that the chain is short enough to prevent the motor jumping off even if the cramp becomes absolutely free. If the eyebolt is elsewhere, the chain may have to be so long that it may prevent loss of the motor, but not stop the cramp jumping clear.

Inboard motors

The thrust of a propeller should be as near horizontal as possible. Most inboard motors are designed to operate at not more than 15 deg. to the horizontal, in a fore-and-aft direction. Because of these requirements an inboard motor has to be located well forward to keep the angle reasonably flat. To help in getting the angle flat, the bottom of a boat intended for an inboard motor may be swept up more towards the stern than one intended for an outboard motor (fig. 44A). For this reason, some outboard boats cannot be converted to inboard motors. An alternative is to use a V drive or an inboard/outboard drive, to keep the motor aft (fig. 44B), but there are complications in design and the equipment may be expensive.

The motor drives through a gearbox coupled to a shaft which passes through a stern tube with a watertight gland and bearings each end. At the outboard end there may be a bracket supporting the shaft immediately forward of the propeller. All of these things have to be lined up. It is this problem of alignment which will give the beginner most trouble.

For a small motor—possibly a two-stroke up to about 4 h.p.—transmission may be by a unit, called a shaft log,

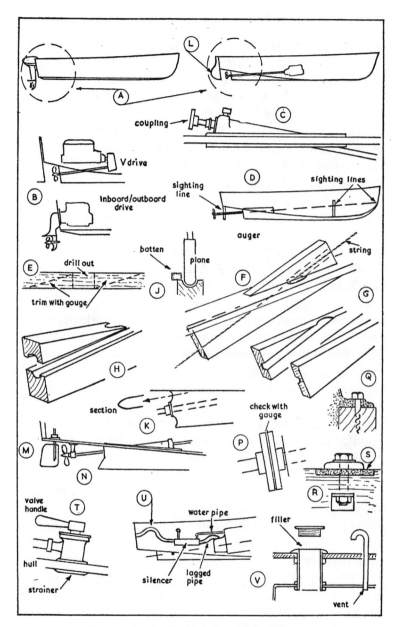

FIG. 44. Inboard-motor installation details

which is a pre-assembled tube, shaft and bearings, which can be mounted on a stout hog, with little additional woodwork (fig. 44C), but for the more usual method of arranging the drive there has to be a skeg outside and a tapered chock inside, through which the drive has to pass. Traditionally, this was bored with an auger, using the outside bracket and a temporary set-up inside indicating the engine-shaft centre as guides (fig. 44D). This was followed by a boring bar with a cutter, which worked through the hole and made it the correct size, in a similar way to the boring bar used in a metalworking centre lathe.

A simpler way for smaller craft is to divide skeg and chock down the middle. A hole is made in the hog and this is enlarged to the elliptical shape that will pass the shaft (fig. 44E). Halves of skeg and inside chock are mounted temporarily and a string passed through to locate the line of the shaft (fig. 44F). The parts are grooved and glued together in position (fig. 44G). In some cases it may be possible, where only a small part of the skeg is passed through, to cut horizontally across the line of the hole, then glue up after grooving (fig. 44H). In either case some of the waste wood can be taken out with a portable circular saw or a plough plane, but final shaping is best done with a 'hollow' plane run along a batten as a guide (fig. 44J).

For moderate speeds the stern bearing may be on the skeg and the propeller fairly close to it, but the wood should be well faired off to give as good a flow of water to the propeller as possible (fig. 44K). The rudder may be mounted on the stern (fig. 44L) or through a bearing in the bottom (fig. 44M). In either case a strip of metal forming a shoe will support the bottom of the rudder and protect the propeller.

If the boat is intended for higher speeds the skeg or keel

should not come as far aft and a bracket is needed behind the propeller (fig. 44N).

An inboard motor has feet for fixing down and their position will govern the arrangement of bearers. For strength and safety, as well as to minimise vibration, the bearers should be substantial and carried as far fore and aft as is reasonably possible. The load should be transferred to frames and other structural parts, rather than directly against the skin. This means fairing to the skin, but also arranging accurate joints to take the main load where other structural members are crossed. Lateral members bracketed or halved into the main bearers are also needed.

Lining up motor and shaft is important. With both in position, but the coupling unbolted, a feeler gauge should be used between the parts of the coupling, then the motor adjusted with packings (fig. 44P). As the boat may alter its shape slightly when afloat, this is best done with the boat normally loaded and floating. Coach screws are sometimes used for fixing down small engines (fig. 44Q), but bolting through is better (fig. 44R). The load should be spread over the comparatively soft wood with metal strips (fig. 44S).

The cooling water is usually drawn in through a skin fitting in the bottom of the boat. This should have a close-fitting hole and be bedded down on jointing compound. The fitting should have a screw-down valve for closing when the boat is out of use, so the fitting should be in an accessible position (fig. 44T).

The exhaust system includes a silencer and may take the ejected cooling water. One problem is the prevention of water getting back into the engine. An upward loop is usually incorporated (fig. 44U). Plenty of asbestos string lagging is needed near woodwork.

Fuel is usually fed to the motor by gravity. Tanks, pipes

and fittings intended for use afloat should be used, rather than ex-car parts. Fillers should be arranged on deck so that any spilled fuel does not get inside the boat and vents should also be to the open air (fig. 44v). Apart from fire hazard, a very slight smell of petrol increases any inclination to seasickness considerably.

Electrical equipment suffers in a damp atmosphere. Insulation of the motor electrical equipment should be above suspicion. If the motor has electrical starting there should also be hand starting, in a position where it can be used without difficulty. Motor and accessory manufacturers provide the equipment for remote control of the engine, but in a small boat the engine can be boxed in and controls mounted on the aft side. Ventilation is important. In an open boat there will be sufficient draught to clear dangerous gases, but if the motor is enclosed or under the cockpit floor there should be a proper ventilation system. Of course, if the motor is air cooled a constantly changing supply of air is necessary in any case. The engine compartment should be bulkheaded off from the accommodation and ventilators arranged to admit and extract air, with a pipe from the extraction ventilator taken low down (fig. 45A). There are many types of ventilator available and types will have to be chosen which do not obstruct deck space. Half-ventilators can be fixed up the sides of cabin or coaming (fig. 45B).

Gas

Bottled gas is convenient for cooking and will give a good light. In most British installations the gas is butane, although for some equipment it can be propane. Both are sold under several trade names, and both are dangerous if allowed to leak into the boat. The gas is heavy

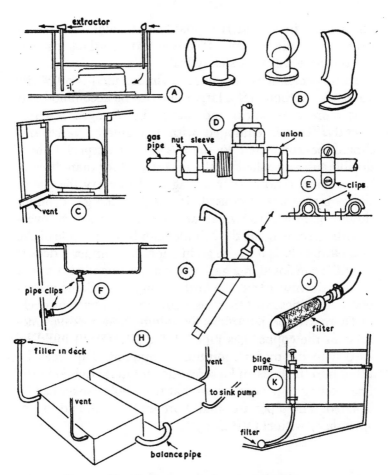

FIG. 45. Ventilation, gas and water installations

and may sink into the bilges. Normal ventilation may not remove it and forced draught may be needed. A small quantity of the gas is explosive and dangerous to life. Consequently, proper installation is important. When recommended equipment is properly used, gas is satisfactory for cooking, lighting and heating. The use of a gas refrigerator in a boat is probably not advisable. It depends on a pilot flame. If this is extinguished for any reason there will be a steady leak.

In the smallest boats the gas cylinder used is often the 10 lb. size, although if a larger one can be accommodated it is more economical and has to be changed less frequently. This is equipped with a regulator valve and should be connected to the system by a special short flexible tube, supplied by the makers, rather than directly to the fairly rigid copper tubing used to carry the gas to the points where it is used. If possible, the gas cylinder should be in a place where any leaking gas will go overboard. In some boats the cylinder can be at one side of the outboard well. If it has to go in a locker or under a deck it should be enclosed in a gas-tight compartment with a vent sloping downwards at the bottom (fig. 45c). Some waterway authorities insist that gas cylinders are carried on deck.

There are special unions for joining and making junctions in the copper gas pipes (fig. 45D). They should be used with the maker's jointing compound. Taps may be fitted into the lines and a screw-down tap is advised in the line leading to the cooker, so that the whole cooker can be isolated. The pipes are small bore and can be laid inconspicuously with clips (fig. 45E).

Water systems

In many cruising craft fresh water is carried in plastic or metal containers from which it is poured, but on a family cabin boat water by tap over a sink is more convenient. The only installation problem when fitting a sink is dealing with the waste. Larger ones have domestic-type fittings, but small ones connect to a skin fitting with a length of plastic pipe (fig. 45F).

There are electric pumps for drinking water and it may be possible to arrange a header tank to feed an ordinary tap, but a hand pump in place of the tap is efficient and convenient (fig. 45G). If there is more than one tank there should be a balance pipe, preferably larger than the one used to draw off water, each tank will need a vent pipe, and the filler should be through the deck (fig. 45H). Water is heavy and the main supply should be in the bottom of the boat.

Toilet facilities are often difficult to arrange in a small cabin boat. There is a choice between a bucket, a chemical toilet or a proper marine WC, which pumps in and out through the skin of the boat. There are compact marine WCs, which will be wanted by anyone looking for something as near as possible to what they have at home, but two more holes through the boat are needed and some authorities on inland waters do not approve this type. There are compact chemical toilets, which will provide hygienic arrangements. Of course, they have to be emptied at intervals. If a marine WC is to be installed the makers' sizes and instructions should be obtained and followed, as incorrect fitting can be the source of leaks and other trouble.

Bilge pump

Even when there are no leaks through the hull, rain water finds its way into the bilges and has to be removed. In a small boat this can be done with a scoop or other type of bailer, but in a larger boat a fixed pump is better. A mechanical pump driven from the engine saves labour, but there should be a hand-operated pump as well. If possible, arrange the suction from the lowest point and equip the hose with a large filter that will take care of the considerable amount of rubbish which finds its way into the bottom of the boat (fig. 45J). The size of the pump will depend on the boat, but in a small cabin boat a plunger type mounted beside a doorway on a bulkhead may pump out through the side of the boat (fig. 45K).

Electrical work

Damp is the enemy of electrical apparatus. Lamps, horn and other electrical equipment should be bought from a specialist supplier and not adapted from car or domestic apparatus. However, some caravan fittings are also suitable for boat work. In most craft a car-type acid battery provides the power. Ideally, it is not also the motor starter battery. If the battery has to be taken ashore for charging, and may have to stand for long periods in a state of partial charge, an alkaline battery ('Nife') is better. Fix the battery so that it cannot move about and have a double-pole master switch gear it to isolate it when not in use. Use fairly stout wire to reduce losses from the comparatively low power source. Use heavily insulated wire and keep junctions away from the open parts of the boat as much as possible. Switches and connections which have to be in the open should be proper marine-type fittings.

13

FINISHING

A BOAT, even in inland waters, has to stand up to conditions more rigorous than are found ashore. Paints, varnishes and other finishes which are satisfactory for household use are not necessarily suitable for use afloat. In general it is advisable to only use finishes which the makers say are produced especially for boats. Internal work may be done with other finishes, but it is false economy to use cheap paints on the outside of a boat.

There are several specialist makers of marine finishes and most of them publish leaflets describing their products, how to use them and what they recommend for particular purposes. It is advisable to follow the maker's advice and not to mix the products of different makers. Some advice on the choice of paint is given in Chapter 1.

Nearly all modern paints and varnishes are synthetic, i.e. they are made up from manufactured chemical resins, etc., instead of the natural lacs of many years ago. Apart from a uniform high quality, this makes application easier. At one time atmospheric conditions and changes in temperature could seriously affect the result. While ideal conditions should still be welcomed, something less than the best can be tolerated and reasonable results achieved.

The sequence of treatment of new work is: prepare,

prime, stop and fill, undercoat and finish coats. In some cases more than one coat of primer and undercoat are given. Although it is the finish coat which is seen, it is the preliminary work leading up to it which controls the quality of the finish.

Preparation

New wood should be thoroughly sanded, using glasspaper or garnet paper wrapped around a cork or wood block. If more than one grade is used make sure the coarse scratches are removed by the finer paper. If the wood is to be varnished do final sanding in the direction of the grain. Fine scratches across the grain tend to show up as darker lines when varnished.

If the surface has already been painted, and this is in poor condition, the old paint must be removed. A blowlamp is the professional tool, but in unskilled hands it is possible to burn projecting edges. A gas blowlamp is easier to use than a paraffin one. A flat scraper is used with a pushing action, or a shaped scraper with a pulling action, on the blistered paint. Most manufacturers supply chemical paint remover and this may be safer to use. Follow the directions exactly. Most makes have to be applied and left for a short time, when the paint will blister and loosen, so that it can be scraped off. The surface must then be neutralised or washed off in the way specified by the makers. Varnish must not be burnt off, but should be removed with a chemical stripper. If the existing finish is sound but dull it may be rubbed down and treated with topcoat only, or undercoat and topcoat if the colour is being changed.

Paint will not adhere over oil or grease. If the surface has become greasy, use a de-greasing solvent, either wiped

PLATE 23

Internal stiffening for attaching bilge keels. Bolts will pass through steel strips over the cross-members

The pair of bilge keels which will be bolted on the hull shown in plate 23

PLATE 24

The centreboard case of an 11 ft. double-chine sailing dinghy. This is supported against bending loads by the gang board notched into the two thwarts

An outboard motor mounted in a well of standard size, with rod steering, a lead to the fuel tank and remote control cables for throttle and gear change

The control position of a small cruiser, with cable steering and controls for the outboard throttle and gear shift

on locally or brushed all over. After about ten minutes rinse off with water and allow to dry.

If working on old wood which has lost its paint and become very weathered, treat it first with raw linseed oil, applying several coats until the wood will not soak up more, then wipe it off and allow it to dry before painting.

If work is being done outside, choose a warm dry day. Apply paint or varnish early in the day so that it is dry or almost dry by nightfall, when dew would affect a wet surface. Frost will ruin wet paint or varnish. Of course, wind will cause dust to settle on the paint. Flies and other insects are not such a hazard. If they are left until the paint has dried they may be wiped off without leaving any very obvious marks.

If work is done inside it is helpful to have a warm room, but it should not be humid or have a tendency to condensation. Oil stoves give off fumes which affect paint and slow the drying time.

Brushes should be good quality and looked after. After use they should be cleaned out with turps substitute or one of the preparations sold for the purpose. They may be kept suspended in a mixture of turps substitute and raw linseed oil. If a brush is neglected and allowed to become hard with paint there are preparations which will soften it, but it cannot be expected to be useful afterwards for anything except rough work.

Paint should be stirred before use, but varnish does not need stirring. Some paints, such as metallic primers and anti-fouling, should be stirred frequently during use. Close a partly used tin tightly. If a skin forms on the contents cut this away cleanly before using the paint.

Priming

Household primers are rather thin and usually pink or white in colour. For most wood on a boat it is better to use a metallic primer, which may be pink or grey. This is pigmented with aluminium. It dries quickly and covers well. It should be tack-free (i.e. does not attract or hold dust) in about two hours and ready for another coat in about twelve hours.

This coat has to fill the pores and adhere well to the wood. Brush it in well. First strokes can be in all directions, but final coats should be all one way, either the direction of the greatest measurement of the surface or vertically. On vertical or sloping surfaces work from the top down. When completing a stroke work back towards that previously done and lift the brush as it runs over the previous part. In this way brush marks can be avoided. This is not so important on the priming coat, but adopting this technique from the start is good practice in the right method. To work primer in well, an old brush with worn bristles is best.

Stopping

When the primer has dried, all imperfections such as holes, cracks and scratches should be filled. There are several waterproof stoppings which may be pressed in with a putty knife. The hard stoppings have a slight elasticity, but for places where there is a risk of much expansion and contraction there are flexible stoppings which remain elastic, but their surface sets hard enough to take paint.

Stoppings should be allowed about twenty-four hours to set, then rubbed down. Rubbing down over paint is best done with wet-and-dry abrasive paper, dipped frequently in water. If lubricated with soap there is less tendency to clog. If there has been much stopping or the first coat of primer does not appear to have obscured the grain and variations in colour of the wood, apply another coat of primer. When this has dried, rub it down.

For very coarse grain, such as on Douglas fir plywood, there are facing cements, which are fillers of thinner consistency than stoppings so that they may be trowelled all over a surface, or thinned further and brushed on. When rubbed down they will obscure unevenness of grain.

Further coats

Each topcoat has its matching undercoat, which covers the primer and leaves a matt finish ready for the topcoat. There may be two undercoats applied. After the second undercoat the surface should be as free from blemishes as possible to give the topcoat a chance of achieving a perfect finish.

If the undercoat is thick and stiff, thin it very slightly. The makers recommend suitable thinners, but be careful of adding too much. Stir very thoroughly before starting work. If the paint is too thick, brush marks will not disappear and runs will develop (thicker blobs of paint will accumulate on sloping surfaces), but by the time this has happened the paint will be hardening and they cannot be brushed out. Spreading each brushful of paint as much as possible and finishing back over the previous part is the best way to avoid runs.

After it has dried, rub down the first undercoat with wet-and-dry paper. With some paint it may be possible to go straight on to the topcoat, but more often another undercoat is advisable for the best finish.

The topcoat paint should be well stirred. The brush should be clean and flexible. Spread the paint well, but avoid unnecessary working many times over the same place. Avoid using very thick paint which may mar the surface with runs. If a small sample panel can be done first and left to dry, the suitability of the thickness of the paint can be judged if there is any doubt.

Varnishing

In effect, varnish is paint without the colouring matter. The sequence of applying coats is similar to that with paint, but the same marine varnish is used throughout. The result is to add a transparent slightly golden lustre to the surface. As all details show through, the wood must be prepared thoroughly and have an appearance that is worth showing.

In practice, it is mahogany, either solid or plywood, which is usually varnished in the structure of the boat, and spruce when used for spars of a sailing boat. Dinghies and other small craft may be entirely varnished, but on larger craft it is such things as cabin tops and rails which are varnished, while the rest of the boat is painted. Teak may also be varnished, but because of its oily nature it needs a wipe over with turps substitute or a special de-greaser immediately before the first coat of varnish.

The final appearance is very dependent on the number of coats and the thoroughness of rubbing down between coats. The first coat of marine varnish may be thinned slightly with turps substitute or the recommended thinner, to aid penetration. This is followed by stopping. As the stopping will show through the varnish it should be a colour which matches the wood. This is rubbed down with wet-and-dry paper and a further coat of varnish applied.

For general work a total of three full coats after the stopping stage is advisable.

Good ventilation helps varnish to dry. Warmth helps, but excessive heat may spoil the finish. Damp weather also effects the finish. Air bubbles in the finish must be avoided. Do not stir the varnish and do not brush excessively. Brushes must be clean. They may be kept in a similar mixture to paint brushes, but should be washed out in thinners before use.

Polyurethane finishes

These synthetic resin paints and varnishes are supplied in two parts which should be mixed in the exact proportions recommended by the makers immediately before use, then stirred and bubbles allowed to disperse for about ten minutes. Hardening then commences. The applied finish is touch-dry in about an hour and hard in less than twelve hours. The final finish will be very hard and durable and resistant to boiling water and most chemicals, as well as being much more waterproof than ordinary paint. One-can polyurethane is also available in some makes.

In general, polyurethane finishes must not be used in contact with ordinary finishes. If old work is to have a polyurethane finish, the old treatment must be removed. Follow the maker's recommendations for primers and stoppings.

When applying polyurethane varnish or paint use a broad brush and apply with flowing strokes. Do not cross-brush or lay-off in the usual way. Apply quickly with the minimum of brushing. Brush marks will flow out.

This paint dries and hardens chemically. It does not reach its full hardness for about seven days. Subsequent coats may be applied after four hours and not later than sixteen hours without the need for rubbing down. If the interval is longer, the surface should be rubbed down before applying the next coat.

Painting other materials

The treatment of other materials than wood is mainly a case of applying the appropriate primer. For steel there are red-lead primers. For galvanised steel and aluminium alloys the first two coats are zinc chromate primer. These may be followed by ordinary undercoats and topcoats. Metal may need de-greasing before painting.

Ordinary paint is not very satisfactory on glass fibre, although some makers provide a special undercoat or primer, which can be followed by normal paints. The snag is the greasy nature of the material. It should be etched with a fine abrasive and de-greased immediately before painting. Polyurethane paint is better on glass fibre. It should be used over the maker's recommended primer.

Hardboard may be painted in the same way as wood, except that some grades are very absorbent and a special hardboard sealer may be used first to prevent too much paint being absorbed.

Anti-fouling

One of the problems of any boat kept afloat is the fouling of the bottom by marine growth. This applies in fresh and salt water, although the nature and extent of the attacks vary between places. Some of the fouling is animal, such as barnacles and worm, and this is usually low down. Nearer the water-line, where there is light, the fouling is more likely to be plant life. None of the paints and varnishes so far described have anti-fouling properties. There are harder anti-fouling paints, which may dry and are better for racing craft, but their effective life is shorter, and the rather expensive treatment has to be repeated frequently.

For a trailed boat or other craft which spends most of its time out of the water there is little point in using anti-fouling. Scrubbing occasionally is then a more effective way of dealing with fouling.

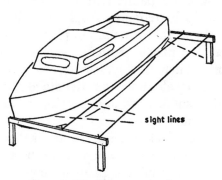

FIG. 46. Marking a water-line

The area round the water-line may attract much plant life and special paint applied there is called boot-topping. If the topsides (the area above the water-line) are one colour and the bottom another, a distinctive line of boot-topping a few inches wide in another colour can look effective. Special paints to counteract fouling and provide this colour are available.

How to find the water-line on the hull of a new boat is not easy. If the boat is easily launched and hauled out it may be advisable to use one paint all over the hull at first, then launch the boat. If it can be left afloat for a few days in most waters there will be a dirty line left at the actual water-line. Points on this can be marked and joined after the hull has been washed off. A design may indicate the position of the designed water-line. One method of drawing this on the actual hull is to set up two strips of wood opposite the ends at the indicated height, then stretch two strings between them. One person may sight across these while another marks the points he indicates on the hull (fig. 46).

Decks and dinghy bottom boards need to show a good surface for the sake of appearance, but they are better if non-slip. There are paints and varnishes available containing non-slip ingredients. Application is the same as other finishes and they are used in place of the other final coats. There are plastic paints in several colours, which can be applied fairly thickly, leaving a rough surface with a good grip. They also have the advantage of a good coverage, spanning small gaps and providing waterproofness with a slightly flexible coat.

At one time black varnish (a tarlike product) was general for the cheap protection of the bottoms of freshwater craft, but bituminous paint is more suitable and is available in a few colours. It can also be used for such places as the insides of centre-board cases, bilges and any hidden parts. Good protection against water penetration is provided by this paint.

APPENDIX A

Boat-building Timbers

HARDWOODS

Timber	Description	Uses
Agba	Light brown, straight grain, wide boards, comparable in strength to Honduras mahogany.	Most parts of small boats, planking, decking. Also plywood veneers.
Afromosia	Yellow/brown, strong and hard.	Alternative to teak for planking and decks.
Ash	Whitish grey, with coarse grain. Bends well.	Not durable, but used for bent parts, tillers, boathooks.
Elm, rock	Pale brown, straight grain. Bends well.	Timbers and ribs, rubbing strips. Not very durable.
Elm, wych	Dull brown.	Planking small craft.
Mahogany, African	Reddish brown. Moderately hard. Coarser than Honduras mahogany. Darkens when exposed.	General purposes, planking, decking, structures. Easily worked. Plywood veneers.
Mahogany, Honduras	Reddish brown, even texture. Finishes well.	General construction, particularly planking.

Timber	*Description*	*Uses*
Meranti	Very similar to mahogany. Hard and straight-grained.	Planking and structures. Durable.
Oak	Light brown, coarse grain. Hard.	Stems, knees, framing. Small strength members.
Obeche	Pale yellow and soft, although called 'hardwood'.	Not durable and only suitable for internal cabin work as alternative to softwoods.
Sapele	Similar to mahogany, reddish-brown colour. Finishes well.	General work, planking, decking, upper works. Plywood.
Teak	Heavy, golden brown, oily texture. Very durable.	Most parts of boat, but too expensive for many jobs.
Utile	Reddish brown, similar to sapele.	As sapele, but considered to be a better wood.

SOFTWOODS

Timber	*Description*	*Uses*
Cedar, Western red	Reddish brown, straight coarse grain.	Durable, but not suitable appearance for exposed parts.
Douglas fir	Reddish brown. Mainly straight grain. Rather coarse. Resinous.	Spars, decking and planking.
Larch	Light red-brown, similar to Douglas fir.	Similar to Douglas fir.
Pine, parana	Pale straw colour with dark streaks.	Not very durable, but a cheap internal constructional wood.

Timber	Description	Uses
Pine, pitch	Yellow-brown with pronounced grain and very resinous. Heavy.	Durable and suitable for decks and planking, but not much used on pleasure craft.
Spruce, Sitka	Pale brown, light weight and straight grain.	High strength/weight ratio. Not durable. Used for spars, oars and paddles.

PLYWOOD

Marine-grade plywood to British Standard Specification 1088 is made from the following woods, which are listed in descending order of weight. Durability is indicated by a number indicating the expected life under marine conditions:

1.   5–10 years
2.   10–15 years
3.   15–25 years
4. over 25 years

Name	Approx. weight per cubic foot	Durability
Utile	41 lb.	3
Sapele	39 lb.	2
Makore	39 lb.	4
Idigbo	34 lb.	3
Meranti	33 lb.	2
African mahogany	32 lb.	2
Agba	32 lb.	3
Gaboon	27 lb.	1

APPENDIX B

Bibliography

There are a very large number of books on various branches of boating, but the author suggests that the following books will be of value to those who wish to learn more about particular aspects of boat building:

Boat Building by P. W. Blandford (Foyle). A cheap book containing some simple dinghy designs.

Boat World (published annually by Business Dictionaries). Information and addresses, concerned with boating, boats and equipment.

Ferro-cement by Bruce Bingham (Cornell).

Fibreglass Boats by Hugo du Plessis (Coles). A large and comprehensive book on the fitting out, maintenance and repair of these boats.

Glassfibre Yachts by Charles Jones (Nautical).

High Speed Small Craft by Peter du Cane (Temple Press). A large book on the design and problems of fast power boats.

Knots, Splices and Fancy Work by C. L. Spencer (Brown, Son & Ferguson). Instructions on a large variety of ropework.

Make Your Own Sails by Bowker and Budd (Macmillan). Step by step instructions on sail making for dinghies and yachts.

Motor Boat and Yachting Manual (Stanford) Comprehensive on many aspects of boating and particularly useful on engines.

Naval Architecture of Small Craft by D. Phillips-Burt (Hutchinson). An authority on the theory of design.

Practical Boatman by Percy W. Blandford (Stanley Paul). Maintenance, repairs and conversions. A companion to this book.

Practical Yacht Construction by C. J. Watts (Coles). The professional methods of building deep-keel yachts.

Sailing Yacht Design by D. Burt (Coles). Design problems mainly concerned with larger yachts.

Small Craft Engines and Equipment by Delmar-Morgan (Coles). Choice of engine and other mechanical gear, including installation.

Your Book of Knots by P. W. Blandford (Faber). The essential knots.

APPENDIX C

Useful addresses

Amateur Yacht Research Society, Woodacres, Hythe, Kent. Concerned with research and development of all kinds of craft.

British Standards Institute, 2 Park Street, London W1. Authority for many standards including those for plywood and glue.

British Waterways Board, Melbury House, Melbury Terrace, London NW1. The controlling authority for most canals and some other waters.

Inland Waterways Association, 114 Regents Park Road, London NW1. Body concerned with access and use of waterways.

Royal Institute of Naval Architects, 10 Upper Belgrave Street, London SW1. The professional body concerned with design.

Royal Yachting Association, 171 Victoria Street, London SW1. The National authority, particularly concerned with racing.

The Ship and Boat Builders' National Federation, 44 Great Queen Street, London WC2. The professional boat builders' association.

Thames Conservancy, Burdett House, 15 Buckingham Street, London WC2. The controlling authority for the River Thames up river of Teddington.

Timber Research and Development Association, Hughenden Valley, High Wycombe, Bucks. All kinds of information available on timbers.

INDEX

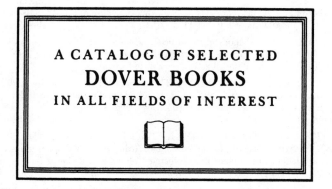

A CATALOG OF SELECTED
DOVER BOOKS
IN ALL FIELDS OF INTEREST

A CATALOG OF SELECTED DOVER
BOOKS IN ALL FIELDS OF INTEREST

CONCERNING THE SPIRITUAL IN ART, Wassily Kandinsky. Pioneering work by father of abstract art. Thoughts on color theory, nature of art. Analysis of earlier masters. 12 illustrations. 80pp. of text. 5⅜ x 8½.　　　　0-486-23411-8

CELTIC ART: The Methods of Construction, George Bain. Simple geometric techniques for making Celtic interlacements, spirals, Kells-type initials, animals, humans, etc. Over 500 illustrations. 160pp. 9 x 12. (Available in U.S. only.)　　　　0-486-22923-8

AN ATLAS OF ANATOMY FOR ARTISTS, Fritz Schider. Most thorough reference work on art anatomy in the world. Hundreds of illustrations, including selections from works by Vesalius, Leonardo, Goya, Ingres, Michelangelo, others. 593 illustrations. 192pp. 7⅛ x 10¼.　　　　0-486-20241-0

CELTIC HAND STROKE-BY-STROKE (Irish Half-Uncial from "The Book of Kells"): An Arthur Baker Calligraphy Manual, Arthur Baker. Complete guide to creating each letter of the alphabet in distinctive Celtic manner. Covers hand position, strokes, pens, inks, paper, more. Illustrated. 48pp. 8¼ x 11.　　　　0-486-24336-2

EASY ORIGAMI, John Montroll. Charming collection of 32 projects (hat, cup, pelican, piano, swan, many more) specially designed for the novice origami hobbyist. Clearly illustrated easy-to-follow instructions insure that even beginning papercrafters will achieve successful results. 48pp. 8¼ x 11.　　　　0-486-27298-2

BLOOMINGDALE'S ILLUSTRATED 1886 CATALOG: Fashions, Dry Goods and Housewares, Bloomingdale Brothers. Famed merchants' extremely rare catalog depicting about 1,700 products: clothing, housewares, firearms, dry goods, jewelry, more. Invaluable for dating, identifying vintage items. Also, copyright-free graphics for artists, designers. Co-published with Henry Ford Museum & Greenfield Village. 160pp. 8¼ x 11.　　　　0-486-25780-0

THE ART OF WORLDLY WISDOM, Baltasar Gracian. "Think with the few and speak with the many," "Friends are a second existence," and "Be able to forget" are among this 1637 volume's 300 pithy maxims. A perfect source of mental and spiritual refreshment, it can be opened at random and appreciated either in brief or at length. 128pp. 5⅜ x 8½.　　　　0-486-44034-6

JOHNSON'S DICTIONARY: A Modern Selection, Samuel Johnson (E. L. McAdam and George Milne, eds.). This modern version reduces the original 1755 edition's 2,300 pages of definitions and literary examples to a more manageable length, retaining the verbal pleasure and historical curiosity of the original. 480pp. 5³⁄₁₆ x 8¼.　　　　0-486-44089-3

ADVENTURES OF HUCKLEBERRY FINN, Mark Twain, Illustrated by E. W. Kemble. A work of eternal richness and complexity, a source of ongoing critical debate, and a literary landmark, Twain's 1885 masterpiece about a barefoot boy's journey of self-discovery has enthralled readers around the world. This handsome clothbound reproduction of the first edition features all 174 of the original black-and-white illustrations. 368pp. 5⅜ x 8½.　　　　0-486-44322-1

STICKLEY CRAFTSMAN FURNITURE CATALOGS, Gustav Stickley and L. & J. G. Stickley. Beautiful, functional furniture in two authentic catalogs from 1910. 594 illustrations, including 277 photos, show settles, rockers, armchairs, reclining chairs, bookcases, desks, tables. 183pp. 6½ x 9¼.　　　　　0-486-23838-5

AMERICAN LOCOMOTIVES IN HISTORIC PHOTOGRAPHS: 1858 to 1949, Ron Ziel (ed.). A rare collection of 126 meticulously detailed official photographs, called "builder portraits," of American locomotives that majestically chronicle the rise of steam locomotive power in America. Introduction. Detailed captions. xi+ 129pp. 9 x 12.　　　　　0-486-27393-8

AMERICA'S LIGHTHOUSES: An Illustrated History, Francis Ross Holland, Jr. Delightfully written, profusely illustrated fact-filled survey of over 200 American light-houses since 1716. History, anecdotes, technological advances, more. 240pp. 8 x 10¾.
　　　　　0-486-25576-X

TOWARDS A NEW ARCHITECTURE, Le Corbusier. Pioneering manifesto by founder of "International School." Technical and aesthetic theories, views of industry, eco-nomics, relation of form to function, "mass-production split" and much more. Profusely illustrated. 320pp. 6⅛ x 9¼. (Available in U.S. only.)　　　　　0-486-25023-7

HOW THE OTHER HALF LIVES, Jacob Riis. Famous journalistic record, expos-ing poverty and degradation of New York slums around 1900, by major social reformer. 100 striking and influential photographs. 233pp. 10 x 7⅞.　0-486-22012-5

FRUIT KEY AND TWIG KEY TO TREES AND SHRUBS, William M. Harlow. One of the handiest and most widely used identification aids. Fruit key covers 120 deciduous and evergreen species; twig key 160 deciduous species. Easily used. Over 300 photographs. 126pp. 5⅜ x 8½.　　　　　0-486-20511-8

COMMON BIRD SONGS, Dr. Donald J. Borror. Songs of 60 most common U.S. birds: robins, sparrows, cardinals, bluejays, finches, more–arranged in order of increasing complexity. Up to 9 variations of songs of each species.
　　　　　Cassette and manual 0-486-99911-4

ORCHIDS AS HOUSE PLANTS, Rebecca Tyson Northen. Grow cattleyas and many other kinds of orchids–in a window, in a case, or under artificial light. 63 illus-trations. 148pp. 5⅜ x 8½.　　　　　0-486-23261-1

MONSTER MAZES, Dave Phillips. Masterful mazes at four levels of difficulty. Avoid deadly perils and evil creatures to find magical treasures. Solutions for all 32 exciting illustrated puzzles. 48pp. 8¼ x 11.　　　　　0-486-26005-4

MOZART'S DON GIOVANNI (DOVER OPERA LIBRETTO SERIES), Wolfgang Amadeus Mozart. Introduced and translated by Ellen H. Bleiler. Standard Italian libretto, with complete English translation. Convenient and thoroughly portable–an ideal companion for reading along with a recording or the performance itself. Introduction. List of characters. Plot summary. 121pp. 5¼ x 8½. 0-486-24944-1

FRANK LLOYD WRIGHT'S DANA HOUSE, Donald Hoffmann. Pictorial essay of residential masterpiece with over 160 interior and exterior photos, plans, eleva-tions, sketches and studies. 128pp. 9¹/₄ x 10¾.　　　　　0-486-29120-0

THE CLARINET AND CLARINET PLAYING, David Pino. Lively, comprehensive work features suggestions about technique, musicianship, and musical interpretation, as well as guidelines for teaching, making your own reeds, and preparing for public performance. Includes an intriguing look at clarinet history. "A godsend," *The Clarinet,* Journal of the International Clarinet Society. Appendixes. 7 illus. 320pp. 5⅜ x 8½. 0-486-40270-3

HOLLYWOOD GLAMOR PORTRAITS, John Kobal (ed.). 145 photos from 1926-49. Harlow, Gable, Bogart, Bacall; 94 stars in all. Full background on photographers, technical aspects. 160pp. 8⅜ x 11¼. 0-486-23352-9

THE RAVEN AND OTHER FAVORITE POEMS, Edgar Allan Poe. Over 40 of the author's most memorable poems: "The Bells," "Ulalume," "Israfel," "To Helen," "The Conqueror Worm," "Eldorado," "Annabel Lee," many more. Alphabetic lists of titles and first lines. 64pp. 5³⁄₁₆ x 8¼. 0-486-26685-0

PERSONAL MEMOIRS OF U. S. GRANT, Ulysses Simpson Grant. Intelligent, deeply moving firsthand account of Civil War campaigns, considered by many the finest military memoirs ever written. Includes letters, historic photographs, maps and more. 528pp. 6⅛ x 9¼. 0-486-28587-1

ANCIENT EGYPTIAN MATERIALS AND INDUSTRIES, A. Lucas and J. Harris. Fascinating, comprehensive, thoroughly documented text describes this ancient civilization's vast resources and the processes that incorporated them in daily life, including the use of animal products, building materials, cosmetics, perfumes and incense, fibers, glazed ware, glass and its manufacture, materials used in the mummification process, and much more. 544pp. 6¹/₈ x 9¹/₄. (Available in U.S. only.) 0-486-40446-3

RUSSIAN STORIES/RUSSKIE RASSKAZY: A Dual-Language Book, edited by Gleb Struve. Twelve tales by such masters as Chekhov, Tolstoy, Dostoevsky, Pushkin, others. Excellent word-for-word English translations on facing pages, plus teaching and study aids, Russian/English vocabulary, biographical/critical introductions, more. 416pp. 5⅜ x 8½. 0-486-26244-8

PHILADELPHIA THEN AND NOW: 60 Sites Photographed in the Past and Present, Kenneth Finkel and Susan Oyama. Rare photographs of City Hall, Logan Square, Independence Hall, Betsy Ross House, other landmarks juxtaposed with contemporary views. Captures changing face of historic city. Introduction. Captions. 128pp. 8¼ x 11. 0-486-25790-8

NORTH AMERICAN INDIAN LIFE: Customs and Traditions of 23 Tribes, Elsie Clews Parsons (ed.). 27 fictionalized essays by noted anthropologists examine religion, customs, government, additional facets of life among the Winnebago, Crow, Zuni, Eskimo, other tribes. 480pp. 6⅛ x 9¼. 0-486-27377-6

TECHNICAL MANUAL AND DICTIONARY OF CLASSICAL BALLET, Gail Grant. Defines, explains, comments on steps, movements, poses and concepts. 15-page pictorial section. Basic book for student, viewer. 127pp. 5⅜ x 8½. 0-486-21843-0

THE MALE AND FEMALE FIGURE IN MOTION: 60 Classic Photographic Sequences, Eadweard Muybridge. 60 true-action photographs of men and women walking, running, climbing, bending, turning, etc., reproduced from rare 19th-century masterpiece. vi + 121pp. 9 x 12. 0-486-24745-7

ANIMALS: 1,419 Copyright-Free Illustrations of Mammals, Birds, Fish, Insects, etc., Jim Harter (ed.). Clear wood engravings present, in extremely lifelike poses, over 1,000 species of animals. One of the most extensive pictorial sourcebooks of its kind. Captions. Index. 284pp. 9 x 12. 0-486-23766-4

1001 QUESTIONS ANSWERED ABOUT THE SEASHORE, N. J. Berrill and Jacquelyn Berrill. Queries answered about dolphins, sea snails, sponges, starfish, fishes, shore birds, many others. Covers appearance, breeding, growth, feeding, much more. 305pp. 5¼ x 8¼. 0-486-23366-9

ATTRACTING BIRDS TO YOUR YARD, William J. Weber. Easy-to-follow guide offers advice on how to attract the greatest diversity of birds: birdhouses, feeders, water and waterers, much more. 96pp. 5³⁄₁₆ x 8¼. 0-486-28927-3

MEDICINAL AND OTHER USES OF NORTH AMERICAN PLANTS: A Historical Survey with Special Reference to the Eastern Indian Tribes, Charlotte Erichsen-Brown. Chronological historical citations document 500 years of usage of plants, trees, shrubs native to eastern Canada, northeastern U.S. Also complete identifying information. 343 illustrations. 544pp. 6½ x 9¼. 0-486-25951-X

STORYBOOK MAZES, Dave Phillips. 23 stories and mazes on two-page spreads: Wizard of Oz, Treasure Island, Robin Hood, etc. Solutions. 64pp. 8¼ x 11.
0-486-23628-5

AMERICAN NEGRO SONGS: 230 Folk Songs and Spirituals, Religious and Secular, John W. Work. This authoritative study traces the African influences of songs sung and played by black Americans at work, in church, and as entertainment. The author discusses the lyric significance of such songs as "Swing Low, Sweet Chariot," "John Henry," and others and offers the words and music for 230 songs. Bibliography. Index of Song Titles. 272pp. 6½ x 9¼. 0-486-40271-1

MOVIE-STAR PORTRAITS OF THE FORTIES, John Kobal (ed.). 163 glamor, studio photos of 106 stars of the 1940s: Rita Hayworth, Ava Gardner, Marlon Brando, Clark Gable, many more. 176pp. 8⅜ x 11¼. 0-486-23546-7

YEKL and THE IMPORTED BRIDEGROOM AND OTHER STORIES OF YIDDISH NEW YORK, Abraham Cahan. Film Hester Street based on *Yekl* (1896). Novel, other stories among first about Jewish immigrants on N.Y.'s East Side. 240pp. 5⅜ x 8½. 0-486-22427-9

SELECTED POEMS, Walt Whitman. Generous sampling from *Leaves of Grass*. Twenty-four poems include "I Hear America Singing," "Song of the Open Road," "I Sing the Body Electric," "When Lilacs Last in the Dooryard Bloom'd," "O Captain! My Captain!"—all reprinted from an authoritative edition. Lists of titles and first lines. 128pp. 5³⁄₁₆ x 8¼. 0-486-26878-0

SONGS OF EXPERIENCE: Facsimile Reproduction with 26 Plates in Full Color, William Blake. 26 full-color plates from a rare 1826 edition. Includes "The Tyger," "London," "Holy Thursday," and other poems. Printed text of poems. 48pp. 5¼ x 7.
0-486-24636-1

THE BEST TALES OF HOFFMANN, E. T. A. Hoffmann. 10 of Hoffmann's most important stories: "Nutcracker and the King of Mice," "The Golden Flowerpot," etc. 458pp. 5⅜ x 8½. 0-486-21793-0

THE BOOK OF TEA, Kakuzo Okakura. Minor classic of the Orient: entertaining, charming explanation, interpretation of traditional Japanese culture in terms of tea ceremony. 94pp. 5⅜ x 8½. 0-486-20070-1

FRENCH STORIES/CONTES FRANÇAIS: A Dual-Language Book, Wallace Fowlie. Ten stories by French masters, Voltaire to Camus: "Micromegas" by Voltaire; "The Atheist's Mass" by Balzac; "Minuet" by de Maupassant; "The Guest" by Camus, six more. Excellent English translations on facing pages. Also French-English vocabulary list, exercises, more. 352pp. 5⅜ x 8½.   0-486-26443-2

CHICAGO AT THE TURN OF THE CENTURY IN PHOTOGRAPHS: 122 Historic Views from the Collections of the Chicago Historical Society, Larry A. Viskochil. Rare large-format prints offer detailed views of City Hall, State Street, the Loop, Hull House, Union Station, many other landmarks, circa 1904-1913. Introduction. Captions. Maps. 144pp. 9⅜ x 12¼.   0-486-24656-6

OLD BROOKLYN IN EARLY PHOTOGRAPHS, 1865-1929, William Lee Younger. Luna Park, Gravesend race track, construction of Grand Army Plaza, moving of Hotel Brighton, etc. 157 previously unpublished photographs. 165pp. 8⅞ x 11¾.   0-486-23587-4

THE MYTHS OF THE NORTH AMERICAN INDIANS, Lewis Spence. Rich anthology of the myths and legends of the Algonquins, Iroquois, Pawnees and Sioux, prefaced by an extensive historical and ethnological commentary. 36 illustrations. 480pp. 5⅜ x 8½.   0-486-25967-6

AN ENCYCLOPEDIA OF BATTLES: Accounts of Over 1,560 Battles from 1479 B.C. to the Present, David Eggenberger. Essential details of every major battle in recorded history from the first battle of Megiddo in 1479 B.C. to Grenada in 1984. List of Battle Maps. New Appendix covering the years 1967-1984. Index. 99 illustrations. 544pp. 6½ x 9¼.   0-486-24913-1

SAILING ALONE AROUND THE WORLD, Captain Joshua Slocum. First man to sail around the world, alone, in small boat. One of great feats of seamanship told in delightful manner. 67 illustrations. 294pp. 5⅜ x 8½.   0-486-20326-3

ANARCHISM AND OTHER ESSAYS, Emma Goldman. Powerful, penetrating, prophetic essays on direct action, role of minorities, prison reform, puritan hypocrisy, violence, etc. 271pp. 5⅜ x 8½.   0-486-22484-8

MYTHS OF THE HINDUS AND BUDDHISTS, Ananda K. Coomaraswamy and Sister Nivedita. Great stories of the epics; deeds of Krishna, Shiva, taken from puranas, Vedas, folk tales; etc. 32 illustrations. 400pp. 5⅜ x 8½.   0-486-21759-0

MY BONDAGE AND MY FREEDOM, Frederick Douglass. Born a slave, Douglass became outspoken force in antislavery movement. The best of Douglass' autobiographies. Graphic description of slave life. 464pp. 5⅜ x 8½.   0-486-22457-0

FOLLOWING THE EQUATOR: A Journey Around the World, Mark Twain. Fascinating humorous account of 1897 voyage to Hawaii, Australia, India, New Zealand, etc. Ironic, bemused reports on peoples, customs, climate, flora and fauna, politics, much more. 197 illustrations. 720pp. 5⅜ x 8½.   0-486-26113-1

THE PEOPLE CALLED SHAKERS, Edward D. Andrews. Definitive study of Shakers: origins, beliefs, practices, dances, social organization, furniture and crafts, etc. 33 illustrations. 351pp. 5⅜ x 8½.   0-486-21081-2

THE MYTHS OF GREECE AND ROME, H. A. Guerber. A classic of mythology, generously illustrated, long prized for its simple, graphic, accurate retelling of the principal myths of Greece and Rome, and for its commentary on their origins and significance. With 64 illustrations by Michelangelo, Raphael, Titian, Rubens, Canova, Bernini and others. 480pp. 5⅜ x 8½.   0-486-27584-1

PSYCHOLOGY OF MUSIC, Carl E. Seashore. Classic work discusses music as a medium from psychological viewpoint. Clear treatment of physical acoustics, auditory apparatus, sound perception, development of musical skills, nature of musical feeling, host of other topics. 88 figures. 408pp. 5⅜ x 8½. 0-486-21851-1

LIFE IN ANCIENT EGYPT, Adolf Erman. Fullest, most thorough, detailed older account with much not in more recent books, domestic life, religion, magic, medicine, commerce, much more. Many illustrations reproduce tomb paintings, carvings, hieroglyphs, etc. 597pp. 5⅜ x 8½. 0-486-22632-8

SUNDIALS, Their Theory and Construction, Albert Waugh. Far and away the best, most thorough coverage of ideas, mathematics concerned, types, construction, adjusting anywhere. Simple, nontechnical treatment allows even children to build several of these dials. Over 100 illustrations. 230pp. 5⅜ x 8½. 0-486-22947-5

THEORETICAL HYDRODYNAMICS, L. M. Milne-Thomson. Classic exposition of the mathematical theory of fluid motion, applicable to both hydrodynamics and aerodynamics. Over 600 exercises. 768pp. 6⅛ x 9¼. 0-486-68970-0

OLD-TIME VIGNETTES IN FULL COLOR, Carol Belanger Grafton (ed.). Over 390 charming, often sentimental illustrations, selected from archives of Victorian graphics–pretty women posing, children playing, food, flowers, kittens and puppies, smiling cherubs, birds and butterflies, much more. All copyright-free. 48pp. 9¼ x 12¼. 0-486-27269-9

PERSPECTIVE FOR ARTISTS, Rex Vicat Cole. Depth, perspective of sky and sea, shadows, much more, not usually covered. 391 diagrams, 81 reproductions of drawings and paintings. 279pp. 5⅜ x 8½. 0-486-22487-2

DRAWING THE LIVING FIGURE, Joseph Sheppard. Innovative approach to artistic anatomy focuses on specifics of surface anatomy, rather than muscles and bones. Over 170 drawings of live models in front, back and side views, and in widely varying poses. Accompanying diagrams. 177 illustrations. Introduction. Index. 144pp. 8⅜ x11¼. 0-486-26723-7

GOTHIC AND OLD ENGLISH ALPHABETS: 100 Complete Fonts, Dan X. Solo. Add power, elegance to posters, signs, other graphics with 100 stunning copyright-free alphabets: Blackstone, Dolbey, Germania, 97 more–including many lower-case, numerals, punctuation marks. 104pp. 8⅛ x 11. 0-486-24695-7

THE BOOK OF WOOD CARVING, Charles Marshall Sayers. Finest book for beginners discusses fundamentals and offers 34 designs. "Absolutely first rate . . . well thought out and well executed."–E. J. Tangerman. 118pp. 7¾ x 10⅝. 0-486-23654-4

ILLUSTRATED CATALOG OF CIVIL WAR MILITARY GOODS: Union Army Weapons, Insignia, Uniform Accessories, and Other Equipment, Schuyler, Hartley, and Graham. Rare, profusely illustrated 1846 catalog includes Union Army uniform and dress regulations, arms and ammunition, coats, insignia, flags, swords, rifles, etc. 226 illustrations. 160pp. 9 x 12. 0-486-24939-5

WOMEN'S FASHIONS OF THE EARLY 1900s: An Unabridged Republication of "New York Fashions, 1909," National Cloak & Suit Co. Rare catalog of mail-order fashions documents women's and children's clothing styles shortly after the turn of the century. Captions offer full descriptions, prices. Invaluable resource for fashion, costume historians. Approximately 725 illustrations. 128pp. 8⅜ x 11¼. 0-486-27276-1

HOW TO DO BEADWORK, Mary White. Fundamental book on craft from simple projects to five-bead chains and woven works. 106 illustrations. 142pp. $5\frac{3}{8}$ x 8.
0-486-20697-1

THE 1912 AND 1915 GUSTAV STICKLEY FURNITURE CATALOGS, Gustav Stickley. With over 200 detailed illustrations and descriptions, these two catalogs are essential reading and reference materials and identification guides for Stickley furniture. Captions cite materials, dimensions and prices. 112pp. $6\frac{1}{2}$ x $9\frac{1}{4}$. 0-486-26676-1

EARLY AMERICAN LOCOMOTIVES, John H. White, Jr. Finest locomotive engravings from early 19th century: historical (1804–74), main-line (after 1870), special, foreign, etc. 147 plates. 142pp. $11\frac{3}{8}$ x $8\frac{1}{4}$. 0-486-22772-3

LITTLE BOOK OF EARLY AMERICAN CRAFTS AND TRADES, Peter Stockham (ed.). 1807 children's book explains crafts and trades: baker, hatter, cooper, potter, and many others. 23 copperplate illustrations. 140pp. $4\frac{5}{8}$ x 6.
0-486-23336-7

VICTORIAN FASHIONS AND COSTUMES FROM HARPER'S BAZAR, 1867–1898, Stella Blum (ed.). Day costumes, evening wear, sports clothes, shoes, hats, other accessories in over 1,000 detailed engravings. 320pp. $9\frac{3}{8}$ x $12\frac{1}{4}$.
0-486-22990-4

THE LONG ISLAND RAIL ROAD IN EARLY PHOTOGRAPHS, Ron Ziel. Over 220 rare photos, informative text document origin (1844) and development of rail service on Long Island. Vintage views of early trains, locomotives, stations, passengers, crews, much more. Captions. $8\frac{7}{8}$ x $11\frac{3}{4}$. 0-486-26301-0

VOYAGE OF THE LIBERDADE, Joshua Slocum. Great 19th-century mariner's thrilling, first-hand account of the wreck of his ship off South America, the 35-foot boat he built from the wreckage, and its remarkable voyage home. 128pp. $5\frac{3}{8}$ x $8\frac{1}{2}$.
0-486-40022-0

TEN BOOKS ON ARCHITECTURE, Vitruvius. The most important book ever written on architecture. Early Roman aesthetics, technology, classical orders, site selection, all other aspects. Morgan translation. 331pp. $5\frac{3}{8}$ x $8\frac{1}{2}$. 0-486-20645-9

THE HUMAN FIGURE IN MOTION, Eadweard Muybridge. More than 4,500 stopped-action photos, in action series, showing undraped men, women, children jumping, lying down, throwing, sitting, wrestling, carrying, etc. 390pp. $7\frac{7}{8}$ x $10\frac{5}{8}$.
0-486-20204-6 Clothbd.

TREES OF THE EASTERN AND CENTRAL UNITED STATES AND CANADA, William M. Harlow. Best one-volume guide to 140 trees. Full descriptions, woodlore, range, etc. Over 600 illustrations. Handy size. 288pp. $4\frac{1}{2}$ x $6\frac{3}{8}$. 0-486-20395-6

GROWING AND USING HERBS AND SPICES, Milo Miloradovich. Versatile handbook provides all the information needed for cultivation and use of all the herbs and spices available in North America. 4 illustrations. Index. Glossary. 236pp. $5\frac{3}{8}$ x $8\frac{1}{2}$.
0-486-25058-X

BIG BOOK OF MAZES AND LABYRINTHS, Walter Shepherd. 50 mazes and labyrinths in all–classical, solid, ripple, and more–in one great volume. Perfect inexpensive puzzler for clever youngsters. Full solutions. 112pp. $8\frac{1}{8}$ x 11. 0-486-22951-3

PIANO TUNING, J. Cree Fischer. Clearest, best book for beginner, amateur. Simple repairs, raising dropped notes, tuning by easy method of flattened fifths. No previous skills needed. 4 illustrations. 201pp. $5\frac{3}{8}$ x $8\frac{1}{2}$. 0-486-23267-0

HINTS TO SINGERS, Lillian Nordica. Selecting the right teacher, developing confidence, overcoming stage fright, and many other important skills receive thoughtful discussion in this indispensible guide, written by a world-famous diva of four decades' experience. 96pp. 5⅜ x 8½. 0-486-40094-8

THE COMPLETE NONSENSE OF EDWARD LEAR, Edward Lear. All nonsense limericks, zany alphabets, Owl and Pussycat, songs, nonsense botany, etc., illustrated by Lear. Total of 320pp. 5⅜ x 8½. (Available in U.S. only.) 0-486-20167-8

VICTORIAN PARLOUR POETRY: An Annotated Anthology, Michael R. Turner. 117 gems by Longfellow, Tennyson, Browning, many lesser-known poets. "The Village Blacksmith," "Curfew Must Not Ring Tonight," "Only a Baby Small," dozens more, often difficult to find elsewhere. Index of poets, titles, first lines. xxiii + 325pp. 5⅜ x 8¼. 0-486-27044-0

DUBLINERS, James Joyce. Fifteen stories offer vivid, tightly focused observations of the lives of Dublin's poorer classes. At least one, "The Dead," is considered a masterpiece. Reprinted complete and unabridged from standard edition. 160pp. 5³⁄₁₆ x 8¼. 0-486-26870-5

GREAT WEIRD TALES: 14 Stories by Lovecraft, Blackwood, Machen and Others, S. T. Joshi (ed.). 14 spellbinding tales, including "The Sin Eater," by Fiona McLeod, "The Eye Above the Mantel," by Frank Belknap Long, as well as renowned works by R. H. Barlow, Lord Dunsany, Arthur Machen, W. C. Morrow and eight other masters of the genre. 256pp. 5⅜ x 8½. (Available in U.S. only.) 0-486-40436-6

THE BOOK OF THE SACRED MAGIC OF ABRAMELIN THE MAGE, translated by S. MacGregor Mathers. Medieval manuscript of ceremonial magic. Basic document in Aleister Crowley, Golden Dawn groups. 268pp. 5⅜ x 8½. 0-486-23211-5

THE BATTLES THAT CHANGED HISTORY, Fletcher Pratt. Eminent historian profiles 16 crucial conflicts, ancient to modern, that changed the course of civilization. 352pp. 5⅜ x 8½. 0-486-41129-X

NEW RUSSIAN-ENGLISH AND ENGLISH-RUSSIAN DICTIONARY, M. A. O'Brien. This is a remarkably handy Russian dictionary, containing a surprising amount of information, including over 70,000 entries. 366pp. 4½ x 6⅛. 0-486-20208-9

NEW YORK IN THE FORTIES, Andreas Feininger. 162 brilliant photographs by the well-known photographer, formerly with *Life* magazine. Commuters, shoppers, Times Square at night, much else from city at its peak. Captions by John von Hartz. 181pp. 9¼ x 10¾. 0-486-23585-8

INDIAN SIGN LANGUAGE, William Tomkins. Over 525 signs developed by Sioux and other tribes. Written instructions and diagrams. Also 290 pictographs. 111pp. 6⅛ x 9¼. 0-486-22029-X

ANATOMY: A Complete Guide for Artists, Joseph Sheppard. A master of figure drawing shows artists how to render human anatomy convincingly. Over 460 illustrations. 224pp. 8⅜ x 11¼. 0-486-27279-6

MEDIEVAL CALLIGRAPHY: Its History and Technique, Marc Drogin. Spirited history, comprehensive instruction manual covers 13 styles (ca. 4th century through 15th). Excellent photographs; directions for duplicating medieval techniques with modern tools. 224pp. 8⅜ x 11¼. 0-486-26142-5

DRIED FLOWERS: How to Prepare Them, Sarah Whitlock and Martha Rankin. Complete instructions on how to use silica gel, meal and borax, perlite aggregate, sand and borax, glycerine and water to create attractive permanent flower arrangements. 12 illustrations. 32pp. 5⅜ x 8½. 0-486-21802-3

EASY-TO-MAKE BIRD FEEDERS FOR WOODWORKERS, Scott D. Campbell. Detailed, simple-to-use guide for designing, constructing, caring for and using feeders. Text, illustrations for 12 classic and contemporary designs. 96pp. 5⅜ x 8½. 0-486-25847-5

THE COMPLETE BOOK OF BIRDHOUSE CONSTRUCTION FOR WOODWORKERS, Scott D. Campbell. Detailed instructions, illustrations, tables. Also data on bird habitat and instinct patterns. Bibliography. 3 tables. 63 illustrations in 15 figures. 48pp. 5¼ x 8½. 0-486-24407-5

SCOTTISH WONDER TALES FROM MYTH AND LEGEND, Donald A. Mackenzie. 16 lively tales tell of giants rumbling down mountainsides, of a magic wand that turns stone pillars into warriors, of gods and goddesses, evil hags, powerful forces and more. 240pp. 5⅜ x 8½. 0-486-29677-6

THE HISTORY OF UNDERCLOTHES, C. Willett Cunnington and Phyllis Cunnington. Fascinating, well-documented survey covering six centuries of English undergarments, enhanced with over 100 illustrations: 12th-century laced-up bodice, footed long drawers (1795), 19th-century bustles, 19th-century corsets for men, Victorian "bust improvers," much more. 272pp. 5⅜ x 8¼. 0-486-27124-2

ARTS AND CRAFTS FURNITURE: The Complete Brooks Catalog of 1912, Brooks Manufacturing Co. Photos and detailed descriptions of more than 150 now very collectible furniture designs from the Arts and Crafts movement depict davenports, settees, buffets, desks, tables, chairs, bedsteads, dressers and more, all built of solid, quarter-sawed oak. Invaluable for students and enthusiasts of antiques, Americana and the decorative arts. 80pp. 6½ x 9¼. 0-486-27471-3

WILBUR AND ORVILLE: A Biography of the Wright Brothers, Fred Howard. Definitive, crisply written study tells the full story of the brothers' lives and work. A vividly written biography, unparalleled in scope and color, that also captures the spirit of an extraordinary era. 560pp. 6⅛ x 9¼. 0-486-40297-5

THE ARTS OF THE SAILOR: Knotting, Splicing and Ropework, Hervey Garrett Smith. Indispensable shipboard reference covers tools, basic knots and useful hitches; handsewing and canvas work, more. Over 100 illustrations. Delightful reading for sea lovers. 256pp. 5⅜ x 8½. 0-486-26440-8

FRANK LLOYD WRIGHT'S FALLINGWATER: The House and Its History, Second, Revised Edition, Donald Hoffmann. A total revision–both in text and illustrations–of the standard document on Fallingwater, the boldest, most personal architectural statement of Wright's mature years, updated with valuable new material from the recently opened Frank Lloyd Wright Archives. "Fascinating"–*The New York Times*. 116 illustrations. 128pp. 9¼ x 10¾. 0-486-27430-6

PHOTOGRAPHIC SKETCHBOOK OF THE CIVIL WAR, Alexander Gardner. 100 photos taken on field during the Civil War. Famous shots of Manassas Harper's Ferry, Lincoln, Richmond, slave pens, etc. 244pp. 10⅝ x 8¼. 0-486-22731-6

FIVE ACRES AND INDEPENDENCE, Maurice G. Kains. Great back-to-the-land classic explains basics of self-sufficient farming. The one book to get. 95 illustrations. 397pp. 5⅜ x 8½. 0-486-20974-1

A MODERN HERBAL, Margaret Grieve. Much the fullest, most exact, most useful compilation of herbal material. Gigantic alphabetical encyclopedia, from aconite to zedoary, gives botanical information, medical properties, folklore, economic uses, much else. Indispensable to serious reader. 161 illustrations. 888pp. 6½ x 9¼. 2-vol. set. (Available in U.S. only.)   Vol. I: 0-486-22798-7   Vol. II: 0-486-22799-5

HIDDEN TREASURE MAZE BOOK, Dave Phillips. Solve 34 challenging mazes accompanied by heroic tales of adventure. Evil dragons, people-eating plants, blood-thirsty giants, many more dangerous adversaries lurk at every twist and turn. 34 mazes, stories, solutions. 48pp. 8¼ x 11.   0-486-24566-7

LETTERS OF W. A. MOZART, Wolfgang A. Mozart. Remarkable letters show bawdy wit, humor, imagination, musical insights, contemporary musical world; includes some letters from Leopold Mozart. 276pp. 5⅜ x 8½.   0-486-22859-2

BASIC PRINCIPLES OF CLASSICAL BALLET, Agrippina Vaganova. Great Russian theoretician, teacher explains methods for teaching classical ballet. 118 illustrations. 175pp. 5⅜ x 8½.   0-486-22036-2

THE JUMPING FROG, Mark Twain. Revenge edition. The original story of The Celebrated Jumping Frog of Calaveras County, a hapless French translation, and Twain's hilarious "retranslation" from the French. 12 illustrations. 66pp. 5⅜ x 8½.
0-486-22686-7

BEST REMEMBERED POEMS, Martin Gardner (ed.). The 126 poems in this superb collection of 19th- and 20th-century British and American verse range from Shelley's "To a Skylark" to the impassioned "Renascence" of Edna St. Vincent Millay and to Edward Lear's whimsical "The Owl and the Pussycat." 224pp. 5⅜ x 8½.
0-486-27165-X

COMPLETE SONNETS, William Shakespeare. Over 150 exquisite poems deal with love, friendship, the tyranny of time, beauty's evanescence, death and other themes in language of remarkable power, precision and beauty. Glossary of archaic terms. 80pp. 5³⁄₁₆ x 8¼.   0-486-26686-9

HISTORIC HOMES OF THE AMERICAN PRESIDENTS, Second, Revised Edition, Irvin Haas. A traveler's guide to American Presidential homes, most open to the public, depicting and describing homes occupied by every American President from George Washington to George Bush. With visiting hours, admission charges, travel routes. 175 photographs. Index. 160pp. 8¼ x 11.   0-486-26751-2

THE WIT AND HUMOR OF OSCAR WILDE, Alvin Redman (ed.). More than 1,000 ripostes, paradoxes, wisecracks: Work is the curse of the drinking classes; I can resist everything except temptation; etc. 258pp. 5⅜ x 8½.   0-486-20602-5

SHAKESPEARE LEXICON AND QUOTATION DICTIONARY, Alexander Schmidt. Full definitions, locations, shades of meaning in every word in plays and poems. More than 50,000 exact quotations. 1,485pp. 6½ x 9¼. 2-vol. set.
Vol. 1: 0-486-22726-X   Vol. 2: 0-486-22727-8

SELECTED POEMS, Emily Dickinson. Over 100 best-known, best-loved poems by one of America's foremost poets, reprinted from authoritative early editions. No comparable edition at this price. Index of first lines. 64pp. 5³⁄₁₆ x 8¼. 0-486-26466-1

THE INSIDIOUS DR. FU-MANCHU, Sax Rohmer. The first of the popular mystery series introduces a pair of English detectives to their archnemesis, the diabolical Dr. Fu-Manchu. Flavorful atmosphere, fast-paced action, and colorful characters enliven this classic of the genre. 208pp. 5³⁄₁₆ x 8¼.   0-486-29898-1

THE MALLEUS MALEFICARUM OF KRAMER AND SPRENGER, translated by Montague Summers. Full text of most important witchhunter's "bible," used by both Catholics and Protestants. 278pp. 6⅝ x 10. 0-486-22802-9

SPANISH STORIES/CUENTOS ESPAÑOLES: A Dual-Language Book, Angel Flores (ed.). Unique format offers 13 great stories in Spanish by Cervantes, Borges, others. Faithful English translations on facing pages. 352pp. 5⅜ x 8½. 0-486-25399-6

GARDEN CITY, LONG ISLAND, IN EARLY PHOTOGRAPHS, 1869–1919, Mildred H. Smith. Handsome treasury of 118 vintage pictures, accompanied by carefully researched captions, document the Garden City Hotel fire (1899), the Vanderbilt Cup Race (1908), the first airmail flight departing from the Nassau Boulevard Aerodrome (1911), and much more. 96pp. 8⅞ x 11¾. 0-486-40669-5

OLD QUEENS, N.Y., IN EARLY PHOTOGRAPHS, Vincent F. Seyfried and William Asadorian. Over 160 rare photographs of Maspeth, Jamaica, Jackson Heights, and other areas. Vintage views of DeWitt Clinton mansion, 1939 World's Fair and more. Captions. 192pp. 8⅞ x 11. 0-486-26358-4

CAPTURED BY THE INDIANS: 15 Firsthand Accounts, 1750-1870, Frederick Drimmer. Astounding true historical accounts of grisly torture, bloody conflicts, relentless pursuits, miraculous escapes and more, by people who lived to tell the tale. 384pp. 5⅜ x 8½. 0-486-24901-8

THE WORLD'S GREAT SPEECHES (Fourth Enlarged Edition), Lewis Copeland, Lawrence W. Lamm, and Stephen J. McKenna. Nearly 300 speeches provide public speakers with a wealth of updated quotes and inspiration–from Pericles' funeral oration and William Jennings Bryan's "Cross of Gold Speech" to Malcolm X's powerful words on the Black Revolution and Earl of Spenser's tribute to his sister, Diana, Princess of Wales. 944pp. 5⅜ x 8⅜. 0-486-40903-1

THE BOOK OF THE SWORD, Sir Richard F. Burton. Great Victorian scholar/adventurer's eloquent, erudite history of the "queen of weapons"–from prehistory to early Roman Empire. Evolution and development of early swords, variations (sabre, broadsword, cutlass, scimitar, etc.), much more. 336pp. 6⅛ x 9¼. 0-486-25434-8

AUTOBIOGRAPHY: The Story of My Experiments with Truth, Mohandas K. Gandhi. Boyhood, legal studies, purification, the growth of the Satyagraha (nonviolent protest) movement. Critical, inspiring work of the man responsible for the freedom of India. 480pp. 5⅜ x 8½. (Available in U.S. only.) 0-486-24593-4

CELTIC MYTHS AND LEGENDS, T. W. Rolleston. Masterful retelling of Irish and Welsh stories and tales. Cuchulain, King Arthur, Deirdre, the Grail, many more. First paperback edition. 58 full-page illustrations. 512pp. 5⅜ x 8½. 0-486-26507-2

THE PRINCIPLES OF PSYCHOLOGY, William James. Famous long course complete, unabridged. Stream of thought, time perception, memory, experimental methods; great work decades ahead of its time. 94 figures. 1,391pp. 5⅜ x 8½. 2-vol. set. Vol. I: 0-486-20381-6 Vol. II: 0-486-20382-4

THE WORLD AS WILL AND REPRESENTATION, Arthur Schopenhauer. Definitive English translation of Schopenhauer's life work, correcting more than 1,000 errors, omissions in earlier translations. Translated by E. F. J. Payne. Total of 1,269pp. 5⅜ x 8½. 2-vol. set. Vol. 1: 0-486-21761-2 Vol. 2: 0-486-21762-0

MAGIC AND MYSTERY IN TIBET, Madame Alexandra David-Neel. Experiences among lamas, magicians, sages, sorcerers, Bonpa wizards. A true psychic discovery. 32 illustrations. 321pp. 5⅜ x 8½. (Available in U.S. only.) 0-486-22682-4

THE EGYPTIAN BOOK OF THE DEAD, E. A. Wallis Budge. Complete reproduction of Ani's papyrus, finest ever found. Full hieroglyphic text, interlinear transliteration, word-for-word translation, smooth translation. 533pp. 6½ x 9¼. 0-486-21866-X

HISTORIC COSTUME IN PICTURES, Braun & Schneider. Over 1,450 costumed figures in clearly detailed engravings–from dawn of civilization to end of 19th century. Captions. Many folk costumes. 256pp. 8⅜ x 11¾. 0-486-23150-X

MATHEMATICS FOR THE NONMATHEMATICIAN, Morris Kline. Detailed, college-level treatment of mathematics in cultural and historical context, with numerous exercises. Recommended Reading Lists. Tables. Numerous figures. 641pp. 5⅜ x 8½. 0-486-24823-2

PROBABILISTIC METHODS IN THE THEORY OF STRUCTURES, Isaac Elishakoff. Well-written introduction covers the elements of the theory of probability from two or more random variables, the reliability of such multivariable structures, the theory of random function, Monte Carlo methods of treating problems incapable of exact solution, and more. Examples. 502pp. 5⅜ x 8½. 0-486-40691-1

THE RIME OF THE ANCIENT MARINER, Gustave Doré, S. T. Coleridge. Doré's finest work; 34 plates capture moods, subtleties of poem. Flawless full-size reproductions printed on facing pages with authoritative text of poem. "Beautiful. Simply beautiful."–*Publisher's Weekly*. 77pp. 9¼ x 12. 0-486-22305-1

SCULPTURE: Principles and Practice, Louis Slobodkin. Step-by-step approach to clay, plaster, metals, stone; classical and modern. 253 drawings, photos. 255pp. 8⅛ x 11. 0-486-22960-2

THE INFLUENCE OF SEA POWER UPON HISTORY, 1660–1783, A. T. Mahan. Influential classic of naval history and tactics still used as text in war colleges. First paperback edition. 4 maps. 24 battle plans. 640pp. 5⅜ x 8½. 0-486-25509-3

THE STORY OF THE TITANIC AS TOLD BY ITS SURVIVORS, Jack Winocour (ed.). What it was really like. Panic, despair, shocking inefficiency, and a little heroism. More thrilling than any fictional account. 26 illustrations. 320pp. 5⅜ x 8½. 0-486-20610-6

ONE TWO THREE . . . INFINITY: Facts and Speculations of Science, George Gamow. Great physicist's fascinating, readable overview of contemporary science: number theory, relativity, fourth dimension, entropy, genes, atomic structure, much more. 128 illustrations. Index. 352pp. 5⅜ x 8½. 0-486-25664-2

DALÍ ON MODERN ART: The Cuckolds of Antiquated Modern Art, Salvador Dalí. Influential painter skewers modern art and its practitioners. Outrageous evaluations of Picasso, Cézanne, Turner, more. 15 renderings of paintings discussed. 44 calligraphic decorations by Dalí. 96pp. 5⅜ x 8½. (Available in U.S. only.) 0-486-29220-7

ANTIQUE PLAYING CARDS: A Pictorial History, Henry René D'Allemagne. Over 900 elaborate, decorative images from rare playing cards (14th–20th centuries): Bacchus, death, dancing dogs, hunting scenes, royal coats of arms, players cheating, much more. 96pp. 9¼ x 12¼. 0-486-29265-7

MAKING FURNITURE MASTERPIECES: 30 Projects with Measured Drawings, Franklin H. Gottshall. Step-by-step instructions, illustrations for constructing handsome, useful pieces, among them a Sheraton desk, Chippendale chair, Spanish desk, Queen Anne table and a William and Mary dressing mirror. 224pp. 8⅛ x 11¼.
0-486-29338-6

NORTH AMERICAN INDIAN DESIGNS FOR ARTISTS AND CRAFTSPEOPLE, Eva Wilson. Over 360 authentic copyright-free designs adapted from Navajo blankets, Hopi pottery, Sioux buffalo hides, more. Geometrics, symbolic figures, plant and animal motifs, etc. 128pp. 8⅜ x 11. (Not for sale in the United Kingdom.) 0-486-25341-4

THE FOSSIL BOOK: A Record of Prehistoric Life, Patricia V. Rich et al. Profusely illustrated definitive guide covers everything from single-celled organisms and dinosaurs to birds and mammals and the interplay between climate and man. Over 1,500 illustrations. 760pp. 7½ x 10⅛. 0-486-29371-8

VICTORIAN ARCHITECTURAL DETAILS: Designs for Over 700 Stairs, Mantels, Doors, Windows, Cornices, Porches, and Other Decorative Elements, A. J. Bicknell & Company. Everything from dormer windows and piazzas to balconies and gable ornaments. Also includes elevations and floor plans for handsome, private residences and commercial structures. 80pp. 9⅜ x 12¼. 0-486-44015-X

WESTERN ISLAMIC ARCHITECTURE: A Concise Introduction, John D. Hoag. Profusely illustrated critical appraisal compares and contrasts Islamic mosques and palaces–from Spain and Egypt to other areas in the Middle East. 139 illustrations. 128pp. 6 x 9. 0-486-43760-4

CHINESE ARCHITECTURE: A Pictorial History, Liang Ssu-ch'eng. More than 240 rare photographs and drawings depict temples, pagodas, tombs, bridges, and imperial palaces comprising much of China's architectural heritage. 152 halftones, 94 diagrams. 232pp. 10¾ x 9⅞. 0-486-43999-2

THE RENAISSANCE: Studies in Art and Poetry, Walter Pater. One of the most talked-about books of the 19th century, *The Renaissance* combines scholarship and philosophy in an innovative work of cultural criticism that examines the achievements of Botticelli, Leonardo, Michelangelo, and other artists. "The holy writ of beauty."–Oscar Wilde. 160pp. 5⅜ x 8½. 0-486-44025-7

A TREATISE ON PAINTING, Leonardo da Vinci. The great Renaissance artist's practical advice on drawing and painting techniques covers anatomy, perspective, composition, light and shadow, and color. A classic of art instruction, it features 48 drawings by Nicholas Poussin and Leon Battista Alberti. 192pp. 5⅜ x 8½.
0-486-44155-5

THE MIND OF LEONARDO DA VINCI, Edward McCurdy. More than just a biography, this classic study by a distinguished historian draws upon Leonardo's extensive writings to offer numerous demonstrations of the Renaissance master's achievements, not only in sculpture and painting, but also in music, engineering, and even experimental aviation. 384pp. 5⅜ x 8½. 0-486-44142-3

WASHINGTON IRVING'S RIP VAN WINKLE, Illustrated by Arthur Rackham. Lovely prints that established artist as a leading illustrator of the time and forever etched into the popular imagination a classic of Catskill lore. 51 full-color plates. 80pp. 8⅜ x 11. 0-486-44242-X

HENSCHE ON PAINTING, John W. Robichaux. Basic painting philosophy and methodology of a great teacher, as expounded in his famous classes and workshops on Cape Cod. 7 illustrations in color on covers. 80pp. 5⅜ x 8½. 0-486-43728-0

LIGHT AND SHADE: A Classic Approach to Three-Dimensional Drawing, Mrs. Mary P. Merrifield. Handy reference clearly demonstrates principles of light and shade by revealing effects of common daylight, sunshine, and candle or artificial light on geometrical solids. 13 plates. 64pp. 5⅜ x 8½. 0-486-44143-1

ASTROLOGY AND ASTRONOMY: A Pictorial Archive of Signs and Symbols, Ernst and Johanna Lehner. Treasure trove of stories, lore, and myth, accompanied by more than 300 rare illustrations of planets, the Milky Way, signs of the zodiac, comets, meteors, and other astronomical phenomena. 192pp. 8⅜ x 11. 0-486-43981-X

JEWELRY MAKING: Techniques for Metal, Tim McCreight. Easy-to-follow instructions and carefully executed illustrations describe tools and techniques, use of gems and enamels, wire inlay, casting, and other topics. 72 line illustrations and diagrams. 176pp. 8¼ x 10⅞. 0-486-44043-5

MAKING BIRDHOUSES: Easy and Advanced Projects, Gladstone Califf. Easy-to-follow instructions include diagrams for everything from a one-room house for bluebirds to a forty-two-room structure for purple martins. 56 plates; 4 figures. 80pp. 8¾ x 6⅜. 0-486-44183-0

LITTLE BOOK OF LOG CABINS: How to Build and Furnish Them, William S. Wicks. Handy how-to manual, with instructions and illustrations for building cabins in the Adirondack style, fireplaces, stairways, furniture, beamed ceilings, and more. 102 line drawings. 96pp. 8¾ x 6⅜. 0-486-44259-4

THE SEASONS OF AMERICA PAST, Eric Sloane. From "sugaring time" and strawberry picking to Indian summer and fall harvest, a whole year's activities described in charming prose and enhanced with 79 of the author's own illustrations. 160pp. 8¼ x 11. 0-486-44220-9

THE METROPOLIS OF TOMORROW, Hugh Ferriss. Generous, prophetic vision of the metropolis of the future, as perceived in 1929. Powerful illustrations of towering structures, wide avenues, and rooftop parks–all features in many of today's modern cities. 59 illustrations. 144pp. 8¼ x 11. 0-486-43727-2

THE PATH TO ROME, Hilaire Belloc. This 1902 memoir abounds in lively vignettes from a vanished time, recounting a pilgrimage on foot across the Alps and Apennines in order to "see all Europe which the Christian Faith has saved." 77 of the author's original line drawings complement his sparkling prose. 272pp. 5⅜ x 8½. 0-486-44001-X

THE HISTORY OF RASSELAS: Prince of Abissinia, Samuel Johnson. Distinguished English writer attacks eighteenth-century optimism and man's unrealistic estimates of what life has to offer. 112pp. 5⅜ x 8½. 0-486-44094-X

A VOYAGE TO ARCTURUS, David Lindsay. A brilliant flight of pure fancy, where wild creatures crowd the fantastic landscape and demented torturers dominate victims with their bizarre mental powers. 272pp. 5⅜ x 8½. 0-486-44198-9

Paperbound unless otherwise indicated. Available at your book dealer, online at **www.doverpublications.com**, or by writing to Dept. GI, Dover Publications, Inc., 31 East 2nd Street, Mineola, NY 11501. For current price information or for free catalogs (please indicate field of interest), write to Dover Publications or log on to **www.doverpublications.com** and see every Dover book in print. Dover publishes more than 500 books each year on science, elementary and advanced mathematics, biology, music, art, literary history, social sciences, and other areas.